BONES ROCK!

AR Level: 6.7
Pts: 6.0   DATE DUE

BONES ROCK!

Everything You Need to Know to Be a Paleontologist

PETER LARSON & KRISTIN DONNAN

INVISIBLE CITIES PRESS
MONTPELIER, VERMONT

Invisible Cities Press
50 State Street
Montpelier, VT 05602
www.invisiblecitiespress.com

Library of Congress Cataloging-in-Publication Data

Larson, Peter L.
Bones rock! : everything you need to know to be a paleontologist /
Peter Larson and Kristin Donnan.— 1st ed.
p.   cm.
Includes bibliographical references and index.
ISBN 1-931229-35-X (alk. paper)
1. Paleontologists—Juvenile literature.
2. Paleontology—Vocational guidance—Juvenile literature.
I. Donnan, Kristin. II. Title.
QE714.7.L37 2004
560—dc22
2004000413

All "Paleo Pete" illustrations by Dorothy Sigler Norton.

Printed in the United States
Book design by Peter Holm, Sterling Hill Productions

SECOND PRINTING

CONTENTS

This book is dedicated to every kid who's ever gone fossil collecting with us—especially Sarah, Matt, Tim, and Ella—and to every kid who wants to collect fossils. That means YOU.

From left, Matt, Ella, Tim, and Sarah—the kids in our family—while digging fossils together in the summer of 2003. (Naidine Adams Larson)

Paleontology is a lot like fishing: lots of quiet time, with just you and the bones. Here, Neal Larson teaches son Leif how it's done. (Layne Kennedy)

A *Tyrannosaurus rex* tooth still in the ground!
Paleontologist David Burnham points out one of
Stan's teeth to a school group in South Dakota.
(Layne Kennedy)

1

So, You Want to Become a Paleontologist!

Have I got a job for you! If you like **mysteries** or **scary monsters** or **getting very dirty,** you could be a paleontologist.

If you like **figuring things out** or **building models** or **making art** or **having interesting conversations,** you could be a paleontologist.

You could be an especially fabulous paleontologist if you have a **good imagination** and can **see problems from someone else's point of view.**

Let's try a little test to find evidence of your future paleontologist-ness: When you see dinosaur movies, do you wonder, Could a *Velociraptor* really open doors? Would a *Brachiosaurus* chew its food? Would a *Tyrannosaurus rex* be unable to see you if you stood very still? Would one really be able to swallow a lawyer—whole?

How do we find the answers to these and many other questions? My name is Paleo Pete and I can help you. I've been hanging out with dinosaurs for way longer than you've been alive. They've gotten to be my friends, especially since I met the biggest, baddest *Tyrannosaurus rex* ever. You probably know her—I named her Sue. After Sue, I dug up six more *T. rex*, and there's another coming out right now. That's more than anyone else in the world, and along the way I've collected tons of cool facts to tell you.

Paleo Pete teaches school outside. (Layne Kennedy)

Lace up your boots, slap on your hat, and come with me. I'll tell you all about the best job in the world.

How Science Works

To some people, science might seem very serious, but to me it's just a fun way to think. An actual moment of science could begin in your own backyard. Let's pretend you've been watching a bird nest ever since you discovered two eggs had been laid in it. First the chicks hatch, and then, a little later, the chicks grow into young adults. You make one simple **observation:** "Hey! These birds look different from each other!" Next, you ask a **question:** "How can that be?"

Scientists don't simply ask such a question and then switch their attention to a peanut butter-and-jelly sandwich. Scientists think of **hypotheses,** or scientific guesses. Maybe, they think, the eggs were laid by two different kinds of birds, called species. Or maybe one bird is a girl and the other is a boy.

Scientists would then look more carefully at their bird subjects. Suppose the feet, wings, feathers, beaks, and faces all look the same. The only differences are that one bird is a bit larger and more colorful than the other. Scientists might decide that so many *similar* features probably mean the two birds are the same species. The *different* features might mean that one is a girl and one is a boy. This favorite hypothesis has now become a **theory**—our best guess.

These two wood ducks show the differences between boys and girls. Which is which? (Dave Menke, Courtesy of the U.S. Fish and Wildlife Service)

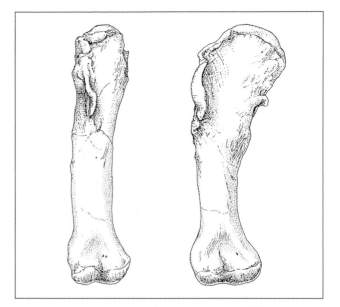

Comparing the upper arm bones from two different types of *T. rex* skeletons. You can see that they don't look exactly alike. (Dorothy Sigler Norton)

Now our backyard moment of science could stretch into a day or a week, a year or even a lifetime. To test our bird theory, we might find lots of facts in the library's bird books. Plus, we might continue to watch our subjects. After a few more months, we might see that the less colorful bird is laying eggs—a girl!—and that the other has started a new nest with a different girl. Our theory is right!

Let's imagine a similar moment of science, only this time, instead of birds, we've found two similar dinosaur skeletons. Suppose they look pretty much the same, except one has thicker bones and is larger all over. Are they two different species? Or are they different versions of the same species—different sexes?

Could we use our "bird approach" to develop and test a theory?

Yes and no. Yes, we can compare these skeletons with all the other similar skeletons we can find. No, we can't make observations of actual living dinosaurs, because they all died millions of years ago. Since there are no living *T. rex* or *Triceratops*, the next-best thing we could do is to observe living dinosaur relatives. Related creatures have some things in common, but let's remember that they aren't *exactly* the same. And yes, we could look in books, but no, not all written theories are correct. Plus we might have discovered something new that hasn't even been written about yet. Finally, yes, we could wait for a long, long time, but no, neither skeleton will lay eggs!

So what do we do? We begin a treasure hunt for information and we piece together an ancient mystery—sometimes a murder mystery!—until we develop a theory. Maybe other scientists will develop a different theory, and then we will get to argue over all the theories.

This process—the thinking *and* the arguing—is what is fun about being a paleontologist.

<3>

Paleontologists love finding leftovers of ancient life. These are called *fossils*. For a long time, paleontologists have tried to group them. I've decided to divide fossils into two types that I think are easy to understand:

Type I: parts of an actual creature or plant, or imprints of their actual parts.

Type II: a track, trace, or product made by a creature.

My pal Leon says Type I fossils are the remains of a *dead* thing, and Type II fossils show us a moment in the life of a *living* one!

What Exactly Is a Paleontologist Anyway?

A paleontologist is a scientist who specializes in paleontology. Paleontology is the study of ancient life—plants and animals usually more than 10,000 years old. Paleontologists also can be *geologists* who study the earth's layers, or *biologists* who study living animals, or *botanists* who study plants. They often have to know *chemistry*—the building blocks of life. And *physics*—how our world works. And *engineering*—the design and building of structures.

Usually a paleontologist has to be more than one type of scientist at the same time. For example, to know why and how a *T. rex* died, I may need to know a lot about the rocks where it was found, and I may also need to know a lot about other plants and animals in the area. To get the dinosaur home, I might have to build things and use some big equipment to move the dinosaur. It's a big job.

TYPE I

- Actual, tiny bacteria, plants, animals, or grains of pollen so small you need a microscope to see them
- Ancient plants, including wood, leaves, cones, and seeds
- The hard body coverings of *invertebrates*—creatures without backbones—like trilobites, ammonites, and insects
- Animal hair, feathers, skin impressions, or organs from *vertebrates*—animals with backbones
- The bones of animals of all sizes and kinds
- An impression of an animal or plant— its actual parts may or may not be there, but we can see exactly what it looked like anyway

Most Type I fossils are not rock copies of the plant or animal, but the thing itself. The real bone, or the real twig, or the real scorpion. When I find a *T. rex* leg bone, it's truly a leg bone and not just a rock in the shape of a leg

Mystery: Paleontology or Archaeology?

It's easy to confuse paleontology with *archaeology*. Archaeology is the study of ancient *people* and what they left behind. *Archaeologists* study how people used to hang out together, what tools they made, and where they lived. As you know, paleontology is the same thing, but it involves studying animals and plants instead of people.

Much of the work in these two related sciences is similar. Both kinds of work involve careful digging with delicate tools, detailed laboratory work, and research. However, humans (our scientific name is *Homo sapiens*) have populated Earth for only about the last 150,000 years. Complex animals and plants have been around three thousand times longer—more than 500 million years!

(See Appendix B for the geologic extinction timeline.)

Animals and plants that die are sometimes buried in *sediment*—sand or silt deposited by water, wind, or ice. As months and years and then millions of years pass, more and more sediment piles up, and hardens into *sedimentary rock*. Because of the short time that humans have been around, only a small layer of the earth's crust contains archaeological deposits. But paleontological deposits can be found throughout the earth, in nearly every kind of sedimentary rock. Since so much more sedimentary rock is filled with fossils than with human remains, a paleontologist has much more stuff to find than an archaeologist!

bone. It can contain all kinds of information about the animal, maybe even evidence of an injury the animal received, or a new part we haven't seen before.

Occasionally, a Type I fossil contains none of the actual object, or only a little bit of it. This type of fossil is known as a *mold*. That is, sometimes sediment hardened around the original plant or animal, and then bacteria dissolved the plant or animal. It's like when you make a plaster mask of your face, but then you take your face out of it. We used to think this mold was always only a rock *impression*, and that the animal or plant was completely gone. Now, using chemicals or ultraviolet light, we can actually see whether traces of the original animal or plant still remain—like if a tiny bit of your skin came off with the face mask. Either way, I call these "impressions" Type I fossils!

As all different sorts of these "actual" fossils are found, we can put together lots of facts about how an animal moved, whether it had a hard life, and even whether it was smart!

TYPE II

- *Trackways* (footprints) made by creatures of all kinds, including trilobites, shorebirds, camels, and even *T. rex*
- Tunnels made by bugs, worms, or other crawly things
- Even poop! (okay, the scientific term is *coprolite*)

Today's chambered nautilus *(inset)*, and a sampling of its extinct relatives. These creatures have chambers inside, which filled with fluid so the animal could change depth. (Ed Gerken)

Brand new *T. rex* skeleton. This Type I fossil is only
partially uncovered. (Peter Larson)

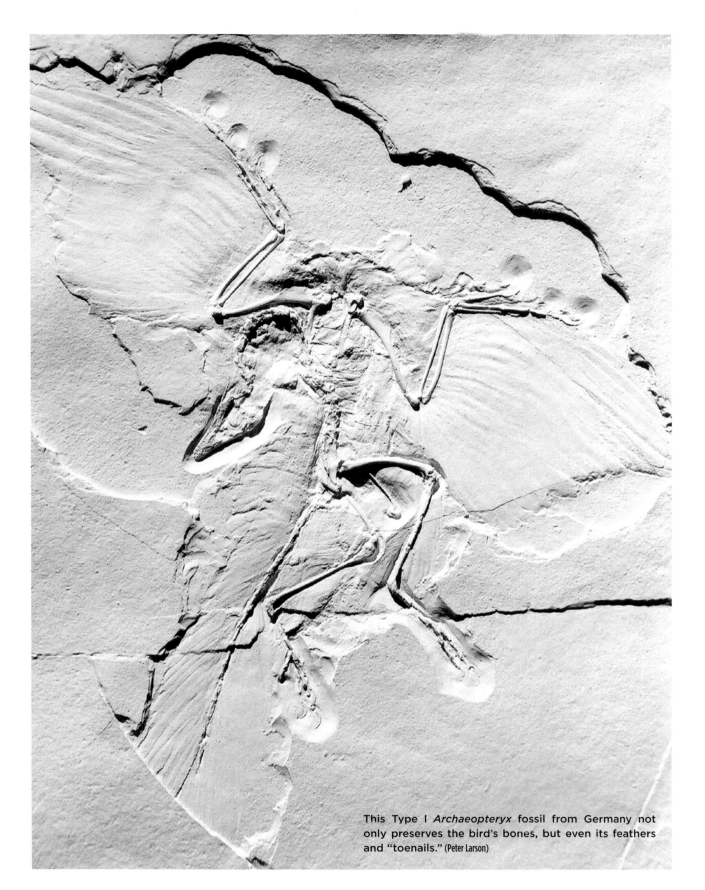

This Type I *Archaeopteryx* fossil from Germany not only preserves the bird's bones, but even its feathers and "toenails." (Peter Larson)

Type I fossil Sycamore leaf from Wyoming's Green River Formation. (Peter Larson)

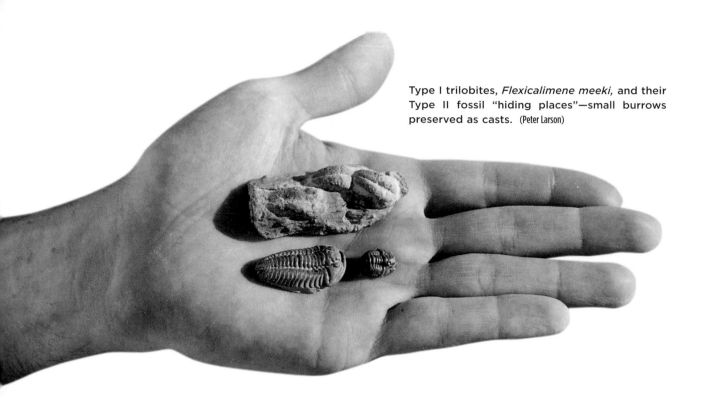

Type I trilobites, *Flexicalimene meeki,* and their Type II fossil "hiding places"—small burrows preserved as casts. (Peter Larson)

With Type II fossils, the animal that made the fossil was long gone before sediment piled on. The sediment hardened over the evidence before wind or water could sweep it away. In my definition, Type II fossils are products made by creatures. We might not even know what creature made a tunnel, or pooped a poop. But we can still learn from these products—and the more of them we find, the more we learn. This is how it works: Picture yourself stepping in mud today, and the footprints lasting for millions of years! That's what happened sometimes when a dinosaur stepped in mud. Using an ancient trackway, we can answer lots of questions. How fast did that animal walk or run? Did it walk alone or in a group? Was it attacked by a *T. rex?*

Mystery: Footprints

Why does your footprint go away within minutes or hours and some fossil footprints last for millions of years? If a duckbill dinosaur (hadrosaur) walked along the lakeshore, why didn't waves wash away its tracks? We're not sure about this, but scientists are guessing that sometimes either the dinosaurs might have stepped in algae, or algae might have grown over their footprints, protecting them from wind or water. Later, after being buried for millions of years, the algae lining would help the rock to separate right where the tracks are.

What new ideas do you have?

< 10 >

Dinosaur trackways sometimes preserve evidence of more than one species. These unidentified footprints were found with those of *Edmontosaurus*, *Struthiomimus*, and *T. rex.* (Peter Larson)

Mystery: Poop

Is poop a Type I or Type II fossil? We could argue either way. Some poop might have bits of actual plants or seeds or nuts or bones or other animal parts. Plus, all fossil poop from meat-eaters will have *phosphate* in it, which is a chemical animals make. These things might make it seem like Type I. But all poop also is a product of an animal—which would make it seem like Type II. What do you think? While you're conducting poop studies, beware of false poop! Lots of times something that looks like poop is really just a rock in disguise.

Will the real poop please stand up? The two specimens at the top are real coprolites—notice the embedded toe bones! The specimen at the bottom is "false poop." (Peter Larson)

Becoming a Fossil

Step One: Preservation
Did every animal or plant that ever lived become a fossil, or leave a footprint, or draw a detailed map to its house? No! Most were eaten by someone bigger, or sometimes even by someone much littler, like bacteria. Sometimes chemicals or even just the wind and rain did the trick.

In what I like to call Dinosaur Country, there's one equation worth remembering:

luck = preservation.

By this I mean that only *preservation*—how a fossil is protected in the earth—lets us find any fossils at all.

When a *Triceratops* died in the Cretaceous period, it might have been well preserved if it fell into a creek and became buried by sediment. And if the sediment sealed out big and little scavengers, and if it had the perfect mix of chemicals. And if no flood washed everything away or broke the carcass into little pieces. And if no passing *T. rex* wandered by and made a little snack of our fallen *Triceratops*. Basically, if conditions were just right, nothing would have destroyed the evidence.

After that, years would pass, and then centuries, and then millions of years. Enough rain would fall, washing more and more sediment on top, and burying the fossil deeper and deeper. Over all that time, the sediments around the *Triceratops* finally would harden into rock. Now *that's* good preservation.

< 12 >

Fossils are being made even today. This elk may be buried by spring floods and preserved for millions of years. (Layne Kennedy)

< 13 >

This is the first we saw of Sue's skeleton. The brown bones poking out are part of her backbone, legs, pelvis, and ribs. They were exposed by rain and wind. (Peter Larson)

But the process of fossil creation—and discovery—wouldn't be over yet. Over millions of years more, exactly the opposite process would have to happen for anyone to be able to find this fossil. Glaciers or rain, or perhaps a river, would have to cut through those outer rock layers, until one day some edge or tip or corner of a bone, maybe a horn or snout or tail, would poke out of the ground. Even with good preservation, a *Triceratops* horn you find today may be chipped and cracked and broken. It's almost too incredible to believe, but it is still there, right where our *Triceratops* left it. When you think about it, it's absolutely amazing that so many fossils are preserved!

But good preservation is not the only requirement needed for our *Triceratops* to be collected and studied. Someone like you has to *find* it first. If no one ever sees it, eventually the same elements that uncovered that horn or snout or tail will break it down to dust.

It's always a surprise and a mystery when you see a bit of bone poking out of the ground. Is this piece the last bit, the only tiny morsel left of a huge animal? Or is it the first bit—just hinting at the rest of the fossil lying safely underground, still waiting for you?

Collecting it is a whole other story, but we'll get to that later.

< 14 >

"Petrified" wood. Although the open cell spaces have been filled with quartz, this slab contains parts of the original tree, so it's really just "fossilized." Note the preservation of a Type II fossil within the Type I tree: insect burrows! (Peter Larson)

Step Two: Fossilization

Most of the time, any fossil bone we find is actually much heavier than it was when the dinosaur was alive. Why? Because of something called *fossilization*, the process that turns a plant or animal into a fossil after it's been buried.

When our *Triceratops* was sandwiched underground, he was not alone. Bacteria and creepy-crawlies wandered through his carcass, consuming his flesh and leaving just his skeleton. Then, water filled with heavy minerals flowed through the ground and seeped into his bones. Minerals love to grow inside any open spaces in bone, filling them and making the bones heavy. The bones are not actually turned to stone, or *petrified*, because they still contain leftovers that were in the living animal.

The Case of the *Triceratops* Two-Step

Paleontology is all about solving mysteries. Sometimes we have a "missing person" case—like when we were looking for a link between dinosaurs and birds. (We found one—his name is *Archaeopteryx*.) Or, it could be a murder mystery—where we search through the sediment for clues as to who killed the biggest *Tyrannosaurus rex* ever. (You'll find out in Chapter 3.) And sometimes it's simply a case

< 15 >

Mystery: How Old Is It?

The earth is 4.5 billion years old. The first saber-toothed cat arrived around 35 million years ago. *T. rex* was alive 65 million years ago. Algae has existed for more than three *billion* years. How do we know all this?

To figure out how old the Earth is, scientists use volcanic ash and chemistry. The ash in sedimentary rocks often contains a type of potassium that changes over time. By measuring how much the potassium has changed, scientists can calculate (with math!) how old it is and how long ago the ash was deposited.

To figure out how old a fossil is, scientists can see how close it is to the volcanic ash. If they already know when the ash was formed, and the bones are right next to it, they must have been covered over at about the same time. They can also use other fossils to do the same thing! How? Most species exist for a million years or less. So if we find a *Camarasaurus* just under some ash that we know is 145 million years old, then we can be pretty sure that the *Camarasaurus* is about the same, and that any others we find will be about the same age as the first one. And this means that we don't even need ash to figure out that bones from any other dinosaurs we find near a *Camarasaurus* will also be about 145 million years old.

Last, but not least, in some cases you can actually date bones directly. In a test similar to the potassium test, we look in the fossil for a rare form of carbon that changes over time. This only works for fossils less than 100,000 years old, so it can't be used with dinosaurs.

Cool Tool—Electron Microprobe

How do we find out what a fossil is really made of? We have to look more closely than we can see with our eyes, and even more closely than we can see with a microscope. Minerals and chemicals react differently when they are shot with an X-ray. With an electron microprobe, an X-ray beam can be pointed at a piece of rock or bone or shell or tree trunk. The pattern created by each one's minerals identifies it—in the same way that your fingerprint identifies you.

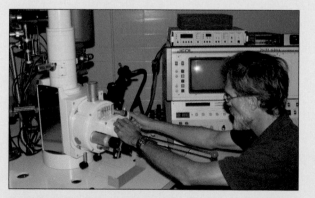

Dr. Edward Duke conducts an electron microprobe analysis at the South Dakota School of Mines and Technology. (Peter Larson)

< 16 >

of gathering more information. Was this *Velociraptor* a boy or girl? How did *Dimetrodon* walk? Who was *T. rex*'s great grandmother? How much did this giant pig weigh? Why does this leg bone look different from the others? Are there living relatives of this creature, or is it something unique? How did it behave when alive? What did it eat? How did its body work?

Most of the time, a fossil can't tell the whole story. We can find many clues, but because each crime scene is millions of years old, cold, hard evidence is limited. Scientists often have several hypotheses that completely disagree.

Take the famous case known as the *Triceratops* Two-Step. For nearly one hundred years, there

were two camps of scientists. One camp believed *Triceratops* moved its front legs like a lizard, with his elbows pointed out. The other camp believed he walked more like a rhinoceros, with his elbows tucked close to his body. Generation after generation of scientists argued about this question.

Each group had developed its theory based on real fossil evidence. They looked at how the leg bones fit together. They looked at how the leg fit onto the body. They compared these mechanics with how living animals' bones fit together, and with how living animals walk. The scientists made perfect models and moved all the parts, as if their *Triceratops* were dancing the two-step. As the battle raged, they wrote scientific papers

< 17 >

Raymond in the ground. (Rick Hebdon)

about it, they gave long detailed speeches, they yelled at each other in conferences, and they made everyone else crazy. Each team's members thought they had the evidence that proved their hypothesis right. They would not change their minds—and they could not change each other's minds. Paleontologists can be very stubborn.

Amazingly, everyone did agree on one thing: they needed one crucial piece of evidence. They needed to see a whole *Triceratops*. Once a complete and intact *Triceratops* was found, it would answer the question once and for all. But that wasn't going to be easy, because *Triceratops* was a very tasty meal for *T. rex*. Most of the time, paleontologists would find the big, heavy, three-horned skull—but often, there was no body. *T.*

rex left only scraps. Even if scientists did find bits of the body, they almost never found the feet. Feet must have been exceptionally delicious. (My dad and brother love to eat chicken feet. They say, "These taste just like chicken!")

Finally, half a *Triceratops* skeleton—named Raymond—was discovered. This creature lay on his right side in the ground, but his whole left side had been washed away. Luckily, all the right-side parts were still connected exactly as they had been in life. This is called *articulated* (the opposite, where bones are all mixed up, is called *disarticulated*). All the scientists on both teams thought that the articulated leg would at last reveal the answer. Can you imagine the excitement?

Raymond's front leg and shoulder—the evidence! Or is it? (David Burnham)

I think the most fun part of paleontology is the sort of thing that happened next. Both camps examined the skeleton. They drew pictures and took photographs and made cast copies of Raymond. They walked Raymond across their desks and across their computer screens. Raymond did his two-step all over the world. Finally it was time to hear the answer.

The lizard group said, "Raymond's bones prove that *Triceratops* walked like a lizard! There is no doubt!" The rhinoceros group said, "Raymond's bones prove that *Triceratops* walked like a rhino! Just look at the evidence!"

Harumph! I was thinking this isn't a mammal (like a rhino), or a reptile (like a lizard), and the way the arms work seemed to show that

Raymond probably walked somewhere in between, with his elbows slightly bowed out. Just like a *Triceratops*. I wondered how we would ever know for sure.

< 19 >

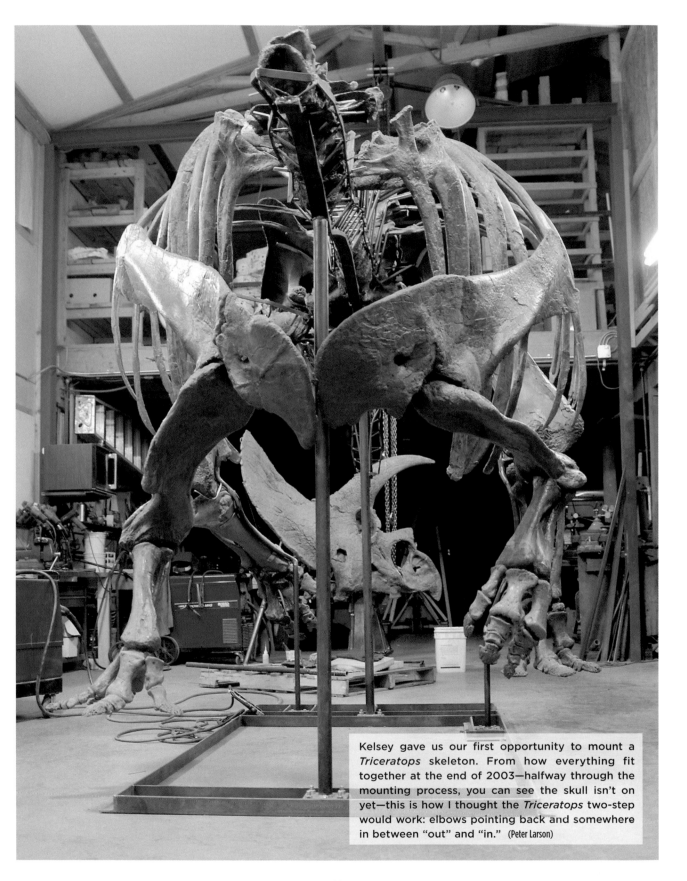

Kelsey gave us our first opportunity to mount a *Triceratops* skeleton. From how everything fit together at the end of 2003—halfway through the mounting process, you can see the skull isn't on yet—this is how I thought the *Triceratops* two-step would work: elbows pointing back and somewhere in between "out" and "in." (Peter Larson)

< 20 >

The very best part of paleontology is that you might be the one to make the next huge discovery. Even if you're eight years old, or twelve years old, you can join the ranks of amateur paleontologists. **Right now!** Here is the story of some kids who have done just that.

Big Bury

The Bury girls know what it's like to find a dinosaur. Chantell, age 11, and her sister Cortney, 10, did it on June 26, 2002. They also know what it's like to have science stop in its tracks and change its mind.

Chantell has wanted to be a paleontologist since kindergarten. Her favorite dinosaur is *Velociraptor*. Cortney's focus is *gemology* (the study of gemstones), but she has a soft spot for *Stegosaurus*. Like the girls, their dad Steve also is a fan of dinosaurs.

For a few years Steve and Christie, their mom, piled everybody into the car for vacations in Montana. Finally, in 2002, they found a place where they were permitted to dig for a day. For about ninety minutes, they poked around and found some random turtle bones—and then: Boom! Bones!

They found a huge dinosaur named Big Bury. Finding your first dinosaur after ninety minutes is a miracle!

The girls spent part of the next summer helping to dig out more of Big Bury, which a paleontologist at first thought was a *T. rex*. Later it turned out to be a duckbill. This isn't uncommon; another famous paleontologist once made the exact same mistake. And still another time, a skeleton was identified as a *Triceratops* and was left in the ground. Years later when I saw it, I said, "Hey, that's no *Triceratops!*" When we dug it out, we met one of the best *T. rex* ever—Stan!

Today, the Burys have not only *moved* to Montana from rainy Washington state, but also have started a new dinosaur museum and summer camp! It looks like these two girls will get their wishes: they can work on all the bones and gems they want.

Big Bury's discovery site—which was first discovered because Mom wanted to take a family photo! She's on the left, kneeling. Third from the left is Chantell, next is Cortney. (Courtesy of the Bury family)

< 21 >

The problem with Raymond was he was squashed. Roadkill *Triceratops*. Although the bones were pretty much where they belonged, still a little shifting and distorting and squishing may have happened. And we couldn't tell the shape of the ribs or where the shoulder blades attached exactly.

Then we met Kelsey. Leonard Zerbst, a rancher pal of ours, found Kelsey—who has the best rib cage of any *Triceratops* ever. These ribs were not squashed or messed up, and when mounted they show how fat (like a hippo!) a *Triceratops* was. The rear legs were bow-legged to get past that belly—but we also could see exactly where the shoulder blades fit in the front. And how the front legs had to move in the shoulder blade sockets.

I'm sure not all of my scientist colleagues will agree with me—because, really, we never all agree all the time!—but Kelsey is my best guess, so far.

The *Triceratops* two-step case shows that although our science changes, often the change is slow. We're always finding something new. Sometimes it's a new part of something we already know, or other times, a new creature altogether. Sometimes a new kind of preservation or technology allows us to look inside the animal in a different way. One day someone might find a baby *T. rex* complete with downy feathers. Or maybe not. No one knows. There's a whole mysterious world of information out there, just waiting for us to uncover it.

Our scientific quest continues. What do we know, or think we know, about the jungles of ancient times? What are we eager to learn? Let's focus on *T. rex* and his neighbors—and his lunch. Let's learn what it's like to collect, clean, and display fossils, along with methods of how to study them.

Now. Could a *Velociraptor* open doors? I'll let you decide, after you look through the evidence.

CODE WORDS

Archaeologist, archaeology	Fossilization	Petrified, petrification
Articulated	Gemologist, gemology	Phosphate
Biologist, biology	Geologist, geology	Physicist, physics
Botanist, botany	*Homo sapiens*	Preservation
Cast	Hypothesis, hypotheses (pl.)	Sediment
Chemist, chemistry	Impression	Sedimentary rock
Disarticulated	Invertebrate	Theory
Electron microprobe	Mold	Trackway
Engineer, engineering	Observation	Vertebrate
Fossil	Paleontologist, paleontology	

< 22 >

Collecting the Evidence

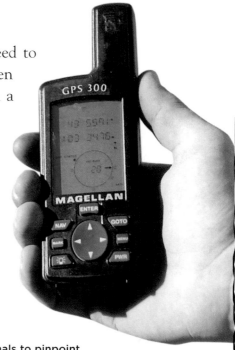

You can find and dig up fossils. All you need to know is where to go and what to do. When you're ready to go out in the field, you'll need a collecting kit with specific tools. You'll need proper clothing and sturdy boots and a broad-brimmed hat and maybe even a *Global Positioning System (GPS)* unit so you'll be able to locate your spot on Earth.

However, to get *ready* to go out in the field, you'll first need to stuff your head full of information. Otherwise you'll be standing outside in the blazing sun—looking very cute, but having no idea what to do next.

The GPS uses at least three satellite signals to pinpoint where you're standing on the Earth's surface. (Peter Larson)

This is how our diggers used to dress. Sam Farrar, Matt Larson, and Tim Larson were pretty goofy when they went fossil hunting as kids. (Family photo)

This is how our diggers dress now, but only on special days. Usually, ties are not required for Matt Seney, Matt Larson, and Sam Farrar. (Terry Wentz)

< 23 >

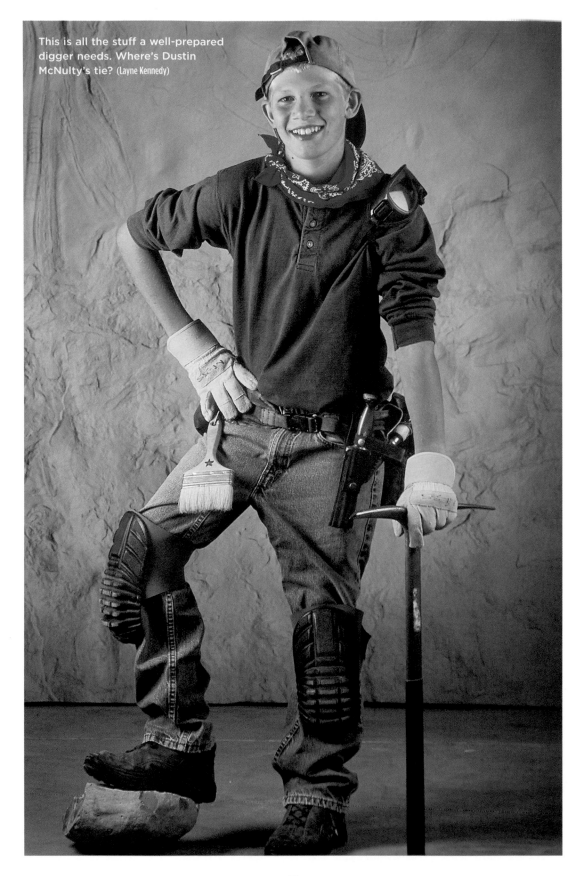

This is all the stuff a well-prepared digger needs. Where's Dustin McNulty's tie? (Layne Kennedy)

< 24 >

Getting Started—Where to Look

Never underestimate your library. Or your librarian.

In the library, we rarely find fossils—except, perhaps, the librarian—but we certainly can discover where fossils have been found before. If you're already a fossil buff, you know where the books are; if you're new to paleontology, just ask the librarian for books on dinosaurs or geology or biology. Either way, check Chapter 7 for some books to start with, and then keep looking on your own! Once you're in the right section, look for books that tell about past discoveries. Pay close attention to the different parts of the country and the world, where fossils are common.

Along with general fossil books, keep an eye out for geologic maps. With a bit of exploration, you'll begin to notice that different types of fossils are found in different areas, and you'll also see how dinosaurs were distributed across the globe.

The colors on geologic maps show formations and ages, and even geologic structures like mountain ranges. (Peter Larson)

< 25 >

Susan Hendrickson looked in 65-million-year-old rocks to find a *T. rex* on the cliff face in front of her. (Peter Larson)

There are four basic reasons why all fossils, especially my favorite—dinosaurs—are not found in all places on Earth.

1. Not all animals lived at the same time. This means that *T. rex* and *Camarasaurus* could not be found in the same place, because the last *Camarasaurus* died about ninety million years before the first *T. rex* was born.

2. Not all dinosaurs that were alive at one time lived in the same places. This means that *Albertosaurus* and *Tarbosaurus*—first cousins—could not be found in the same place, because *Albertosaurus* lived in North America and *Tarbosaurus* lived in Asia.

3. Rocks at the surface in different places on the planet are of different ages. This means that even if *T. rex* lived in Nebraska, the rocks that we see now in that area were deposited on top of *T. rex* rocks. If any *T. rex* are there, they are hundreds of feet underground, under deposits of fishes and camels and saber-toothed cats.

4. Preservation didn't occur everywhere. This means that even if *T. rex* might have lived in a certain place, its body parts might have been washed away by a flood, or dissolved by soil that was too acidic, or blown away by wind.

< 26 >

The best place to look for ancient land animals is near ancient streambeds. In this picture, these kids can see the difference between coarser, sandy, stream deposits and fine-grained silt from the nearby floodplain. (Layne Kennedy)

< 27 >

Keeping these four factors in mind, you can use the maps to pinpoint where you want to look for fossils. Try this:

If you love *Pachycephalosaurus*, you can go exactly where that dinosaur has been found before, or to rocks in the general area that are of the right age.

If your family thinks Mongolia is too far to drive for *Tarbosaurus*, there are plenty of ways to discover what sorts of fossils exist in your area. Start by learning all about your rocks and look for the animals that would have lived near you.

If there was poor preservation where you live, or if you live where there are so many plants that it's nearly impossible to see the ground—a jungle, perhaps—do not despair. You are not the only fossil geek in your neighborhood! Go to your local

museum and learn about its fossils. Join your local rock club. Talk to your science teacher, your scout leader, or the guy who runs a rock shop. You'll be amazed at how many people love rocks and fossils. They will talk your ear off. If you play your cards right, you can get very smart by listening.

For additional Brownie Points, take your parents on vacation to national parks, like Dinosaur National Monument in Utah, or the Badlands National Park in South Dakota. They'll be amazed at how smart you've become, and if you're lucky maybe they'll even send you to a summer collecting program in the future.

Getting Ready to Go

You don't *have* to dig fossils yourself to learn from them. You can study them in museum collections, get fossils as school donations, trade for fossils, or buy fossils. Many people who write scientific papers don't actually dig fossils up very often, but instead they work with stuff sometimes found over one hundred years ago. Others spend time observing living animals and making hypotheses about how a lizard, or maybe a rhino, was like a *Triceratops*.

Between you and me, though, I don't know how they can stand it. Digging is my favorite part.

If you want to dig, you'll need to gather a few essentials:

1. A *mentor*, or someone to take you. Maybe a rock hound or a geezer relative or a graduate student at a nearby university. Make sure you introduce your mentor to your parents! Your parents or your mentor also can help you join a summer dig program (see further information on those in Chapter 7). Please note: mentors have driver's licenses.

< 28 >

When you find a mentor, don't be afraid to ask how much time and help that person can give you. It might seem like a lot at first, but don't worry: mentors love this. Fossil geeks love to hang around with other fossil geeks, and they are happy with any excuse to go out in the field or into the lab. Every paleontologist I know, amateur or professional, remembers the person who first helped him or her—and invites young people along on digs.

2. Permission. Now that you know where the correct rocks are visible, and what to look for—thanks to the librarian—it's not as if you can just wander over and start digging holes. Your mentor will help you contact either private landowners or public land agencies to ask permission and to learn about regulations. *Even if you are not allowed to dig, you might be able to look!* No digging is permitted in Badlands National Park, but after a few hours there, your eyes will get accustomed to what wild fossils look like.

Be very polite to everyone in charge—and mean it.

Top: Paleo Pete and his mentor, June Zeitner. She first encouraged Pete to collect fossils when he was just a kid, and she is now part of his museum board of directors! (May Hubbell) *Middle left:* Pete as a young fossil hunter—with a fossil cycad, an ancient plant from the time of the dinosaurs. This is how he looked at age 13 when June went collecting with him. (Family photo) *Middle right:* And this is how June was when Pete met her, when he was about seven! (Courtesy of June Zeitner) *Bottom:* Pete has become a mentor to adults and children worldwide. Here he is in the summer of 2003 with our webmaster, Kyle. (Terry Wentz)

< 29 >

A well-stocked dig station. (The Toad)

3. Your collecting kit. If you are allowed to look for and collect fossils, it's time for tools. You can put everything you need in a backpack or fanny pack, or when you're an expert, a tool belt (these look very cool). Since some of the tools can be dangerous, see Number 1 above. *Ask your mentor to help choose your tools. And always take an adult collecting with you.* There is nothing funny about getting hurt out in the middle of nowhere.

Believe me, I know about this. I've seen lots of people hurt themselves with tools. But you can get hurt when it seems as if there's no danger at all. I once took too long a step down a cliff while carrying a heavy pack. My ankle sprained badly, and by the time I limped two miles back to my truck—using my pick as a cane—the ankle was already bruised black. I took off my boot—and couldn't put it back on for two weeks. My collecting partner that day drove us home. If I had been hurt badly enough where I couldn't walk at all, and if I had been alone, I would have been in a very dangerous situation. *Never go collecting by yourself!*

< 30 >

First-Stage Kit	Expert Kit	Super-Deluxe Kit
Water	Water	Water
Paint brush(es)	Paint brush(es)	Paint brush(es)
Digging knife	Digging knife	Digging knife
Dull X-acto knife	Dull X-acto knife	Dull X-acto knife
Aluminum foil	Aluminum foil	Aluminum foil
Masking & strapping tape	Masking & strapping tape	Masking & strapping tape
Newspaper	Newspaper	Newspaper
Locking plastic bags	Locking plastic bags	Locking plastic bags
Superglue (or Elmer's)	Superglue	Superglue
Map	Map	Map
Field Notebook	Field Notebook	Field Notebook
Pen & marker	Pen & marker	Pen & marker
Camera	Camera	Camera
First-aid kit	First-aid kit	First-aid kit
	Scribes	Scribes
	Rock pick	Rock pick
	Plaster bandages	Plaster bandages
	More water	More water
	Extra carrying bag	Extra carrying bag
	More glue options	More glue options
	GPS	GPS
	Ultraviolet light	Ultraviolet light
	Mapping grid	Mapping grid
		Plaster & burlap
		Truck
		Valid driver's license
		Paleontologist pals
		Lease for good quarry
		Jackhammer
		Ropes
		Wooden splints
		Boards
		Bobcat earthmover
		College degree (it never hurts)

The more experienced you get, the more stuff you'll need. Your mentor will know when to add items.

Some items from a First-Stage Digging Kit. (Peter Larson)

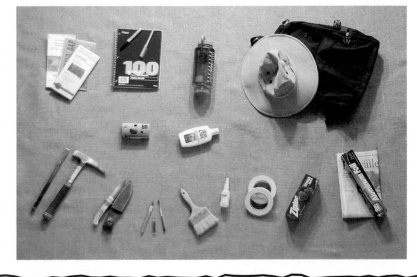

< 31 >

Bobcats are used to remove layers of sediment above the fossil layer—and also to move heavy fossils. Here, people have to add their weight to counterbalance the heavy block. (Dan Counter)

My daughter Sarah uses a jackhammer from a Super-Deluxe Digging Kit to break up some pretty hard Jurassic rock at a *Camarasaurus* site. (Terry Wentz)

What It's Like to Look for Fossils and How to Do It Yourself

Sometimes life's evidence comes as a complete skeleton. Maybe a *Gorgosaurus* with his neck, back, and tail death-arched in the shape of a G, head thrown against the center of the spine, jaws open in a final scream, preserved down to the very last tiny vertebra of the tail. Call me right away if you find one of those, because I'd love to see it.

Paleontologists live for a discovery like that. But most of the time, what we find of an extinct animal or plant is only a small portion of the original organism, an isolated bone, a leaf, the imprint of a patch of skin. To find these things, your eyes have to be trained to tell the difference between bone bits and rock bits. Once you get the hang of it, you'll never look at the ground the same way again.

You can start practicing at your very own house. If you have a gravel driveway or a creek, you may find some excellent fossils right under your nose. Road ditches or places where building is beginning often have exposed treasures. It's hard to find fossils where the ground is

< 32 >

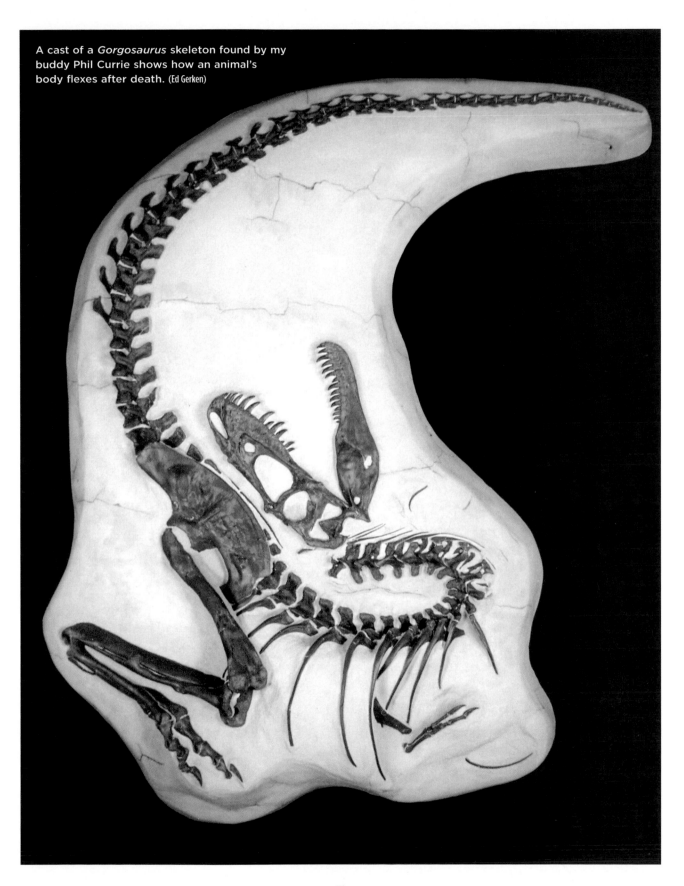

A cast of a *Gorgosaurus* skeleton found by my buddy Phil Currie shows how an animal's body flexes after death. (Ed Gerken)

< 33 >

Who Owns Fossils?

In general, the owner of the land owns the fossils found there. That might be a rancher or farmer, or it might be the county or state or federal government. Before going onto someone's property, you *must* ask for and receive permission.

Things the landowner needs to know: Who are you? What do you want to do? What do you intend to do with the fossils if you collect some? Are you doing a science fair project? Do you want to start your own collection? (See Appendix C for a form you can copy and fill out for the rancher.)

Private landowners usually allow you to keep or buy the fossils you collect, but not always. Sometimes they would like to keep some, too, but even in these cases you have earned great experience and maybe made some new friends. Always check out all arrangements before you dig.

On land owned by the U.S. government, today diggers might be able to dig up and "keep" fossils they collect—but the government might still technically own them. These issues are complicated and Congress is trying to figure everything out. So make sure you ask plenty of questions, because things are changing. Also, find out what laws your state has about fossil collection.

Keep in mind: it's perfectly okay to buy fossils from rock shops or museum gift shops.

covered by grass, trees, pavement, or houses, so look where rocks are exposed. In all these cases, ask permission, be careful, and if you stray from your driveway, take your mentor!

By the time you're making your first trip to the field, you might already know the names and ages of sediments where you're going to look. Are you collecting in the Hell Creek Formation? The Ripley Formation? Is it an Oligocene Age area with oreodonts (ancient camel-like creatures), or an ancient peat bog with mastodons (ancient elephant-like creatures)? You'll get used to telling the differences in color from one sediment layer to another. The fossil-rich light green or maroon Morrison Formation, where long-necks (sauropods) and *Stegosaurus* can be found, is sandwiched between beige layers with ammonites and brown layers with dinosaur tracks.

Your mentor will be able to point out where the sediment actually tells a story. The striped colors and textures in the Badlands' sand castles are a dusty record of fierce rain storms or floods that might have buried carcasses quickly. Their pastel greens, pinks, reds, yellows, and beiges eventually look like road signs to the trained eye. While luck plays a part in finding fossils, experience puts a paleontologist in the right place to get lucky. Time in the field is the best dinosaur divining rod there is.

At first that field time is spent walking. On scouting days, usually I walk ten miles or more at a stretch in the hot sun. I look in gullies, clamber up and down hills, scale cliffs, cross ravines. I love this part of being a paleontologist. It can be tiring, but you can consider the chance for life on Mars or whether Pat likes you while your eyes flash back and forth, back and

Cretaceous sediments may hide dinosaur skeletons. (Peter Larson)

Construction crews often uncover fossils at work sites.
(Peter Larson)

For a paleontologist, reading the layers of sediments
becomes as natural as reading the pages of a book.
(Layne Kennedy)

< 35 >

Tiny dinosaur and crocodile fossils can be found by sifting with a screen at a microsite.
(Peter Larson)

Mystery: What's in a Name

Why are some fossil names written in italics and capitalized, like *Tyrannosaurus rex* and *Triceratops*, while others aren't? Why do we write "oreodont," and "ammonites," and even "tyrannosaur" with no excitement added? The fancy ones are formal, scientific names written in Greek and Latin. The first word is the *genus* and the second is the *species*, and they indicate the position on the family tree each animal occupies.

Other names are not capitalized or in italics. They are general group names. You could say my group name is "paleontologist" and my formal name is *Paleo Pete*. "Ammonite" is a group name, as is "oreodont." Under the group name "tyrannosaurs" are *T. rex*, *Gorgosaurus*, *Albertosaurus*, *Desplatosaurus*, *Nanotyrannus*, *Electrosaurus*, *Tarbosaurus*, and others. Each of them has two names, but often, as above, we list only the genus name. Except with *T. rex*. Since *Tyrannosaurus rex* includes the group name "tyrannosaur," we've shortened it to *T. rex*—which sounds cooler, anyway. Usually, though, the species name comes in handy only when we're getting really specific.

< 36 >

People get on hands and knees to see the tiny fossils in a microsite. (Layne Kennedy)

forth, picking out fragments of bone and watching for rattlesnakes.

Some of the best practice spots—where you can get excellent results—are also some of my favorites. These are *microsites*, concentrations of teeny, tiny fossils. On my hands and knees, I search for teeth or shells. Another way to find these small treasures is to scoop a bucketful of the "dirt," take it home, and wash it through a screen. This is an excellent project that I can start in the summer and play with all winter, when there's too much snow to hunt for fossils. It's also a good project for volunteers who want to learn to train their eyes.

The only way to find fossils is to spend the time looking. You'll develop your own rhythm, your own pace. You'll pick up blobs of dirt and swear they're fossils. You'll pick up fossils and think they're rocks. Here are some clues. Most fossils have a slightly different color than the surrounding dirt. Fossil bone has the same texture, inside and out, as the steak or chicken bones you see at dinner. With practice, you'll begin to see the little polka dots of bone marrow, or the tiny lines of cracks in bone. Your brain will begin to see shapes in the fragments, and you'll guess, "Hey, this looks like the back of a rat skull," or "Look! A *Triceratops* frill!" (A *frill* is that big collar a *Triceratops* wears.) Your mentor will come in handy at this point, correcting you and encouraging you and telling you the truth: "Nice try, but that's a hub cap."

< 37 >

The Sacrison Boys

Stan Sacrison in 1992 with his nephews Drew, Finn, and Ian. (Courtesy of Ginger Sacrison)

Finn, Drew, and Ian Sacrison come from one of the most famous modern dinosaur-hunting families in the world. It all started sometime in the 1960s, when their uncle Stan found his first *Triceratops* vertebra. He was eight. He never stopped "kicking around the prairie" looking for bones—and in 1987 he found his first of two *T. rex*, named Stan after him. A few years later came Duffy, and with that Stan Sacrison became the first person ever to find *T. rex* in two different spots.

But nobody can beat what would happen then: Steve—Stan's twin brother, and the boys' dad—found *another T. rex!*

You can probably imagine what it was like to grow up with Stan and Steve as your uncle and your dad. Finn, Drew, and Ian spent their summers in the prairie and their winters in a garage watching Stan clean bones. The young brothers learned fast—how to tell a rock from a bone, what different bones from different creatures look like, where to look for what. They spent entire days on their bellies, faces just above microsites, picking out the teeniest jaw bones and teeth. They found lizard, frog, and turtle parts, and teeth from *Nanotyrannus*, *T. rex*, *Triceratops*, and the duckbill *Edmontosaurus*.

The boys also spent lots of time at our *T. rex* dig sites, helping uncover bones. All three of them thought fossil hunting was "pretty much the coolest thing," according to Ian. And each boy had his own specialty. Finn was nine in 1992 when he took a trek with Stan, Steve, and me. With his well-trained eyes, Finn spotted half of a large chunk of *amber*, or fossilized sap. Ten months later, Steve walked the same route, and found the other half! The amber is about the size and shape of a chocolate-chip cookie, making it one of the largest pieces of Cretaceous amber ever found. Finn also spotted a *Triceratops* that included most of the skull and parts of the body. Because of its excellent horns and *brain case*, the section of the skull that held the brain, this one might tell us about shock absorption, which *Triceratops* needed to keep from going nutty when it crashed horns with other *Triceratops*.

< 38 >

Drew loved microsites best, and also driving his dad's Bobcat. Even as a little kid, he could move dirt from a dig site better than many grown-ups. Ian's favorite fossil pastime is the actual digging part. He has found some cool stuff—like a great lizard jaw when he was about nine—but mostly he's the digger and not the finder. He's such a careful digger, I trust him with the most delicate bones, like *T. rex* teeth.

All the boys, who are now 19, 16, and 14, and good mentors, agree on a few important things. "Find people who know what they're doing, and go with them," Drew says. "And don't get discouraged, or be afraid to ask questions," Finn adds.

Finn and Steve Sacrison with their amber discovery. (Peter Larson) *Inset:* **The two halves fit together perfectly.** (Peter Larson)

Paleo Pete digging with an 11-year-old, expert-digger Ian, in 1999. (Courtesy of Ginger Sacrison)

< 39 >

Digging!

Okay, you've found something: a bunch of fragments, maybe an inch square each. There are about fifteen of them. At the bottom of a small cliff. What do you do?

Use Your Eyes

1. Don't jump all over the place. You might step on something you haven't seen yet.

2. Look uphill from the fragments—do you see more of the fossil poking out? The fragments had to come from somewhere, and most likely rain, wind, or frost has broken them off and moved them downhill.

3. Once you find the fossil, holler at your mentor to help with identification.

4. If it's something cool, take pictures with your camera before you touch anything.

5. In your notebook, write a description of everything you see. Remember to tell about what the sediment looks like, where you are, and how the fossil is positioned. Ask your mentor to fill in whatever scientific information she knows at this point.

Now you're ready to dig. I can tell you some secrets to good digging, but you'll definitely have to watch someone with experience, and practice yourself. A few rules will keep you from disaster.

Use Your Hands

1. Carefully collect the fragments you first found and put them in a locking plastic bag. More than one if necessary.

2. Using your digging knife, start removing sediment several inches from the fossil—don't jab right at it. Remove excess dirt or rock *above* and *around* the fossil first, not *below*, because it might collapse.

3. As you remove any dirt, check for fossil bits before you pitch the dirt away. The fossil may be bigger than you thought!

4. Sometimes the difference is very small between how the fossil looks and how the sediment looks. Use your brush to keep the area clean so you can see clearly.

Matt Larson when he was a kid, picking up fragments before digging around a dinosaur bone. (Peter Larson)

Keeping the fossil clear of debris is one of the best habits a digger can develop. (Layne Kennedy)

< 40 >

Alexandra Burkot is digging above the bones, exposing them without making them too wiggly.
(Terry Wentz)

< 41 >

Mystery: Glue

The glues most paleontologists use today are high-quality superglues called *cyanoacrylates*. They are amazing because they react with the water found in all fossils, and in *seconds* form a permanent bond. The thinnest variety will slither into hairline cracks invisible to the naked eye! Inside the bone, it will fill pore spaces, hardening the bone so it won't break as easily. Because it is so thin, you can't really control where the thin glue goes, which is why it's easy to accidentally glue too much—including yourself. Be careful. Thicker varieties can stick larger pieces of bone together, and are easier to deal with.

Other sealants, such as *polyvinyl acetate*, are also excellent for coating and protecting a fossil. PVA, as it's called, is easier than superglue to remove in the laboratory—in case a gluer gets overly enthusiastic in the field. To remove all of these things, we use *acetone* or other solvents. Please ask for help with all of these chemicals! They can be dangerous.

One safe alternative that can be bought in any store is regular-old Elmer's school glue. In full strength, it can be used to glue broken pieces of fossils together, both in the field and in the lab. If you thin it with water, you can use it like PVA, as a thin coating to help hold the fossil together. Elmer's isn't as permanent—which might be good until you know what you're doing. It's good as a "starting" glue.

5. When you get close to the bone, use your X-acto knife, and make sure that the sharp part of its blade *never touches the fossil*. For extra safety, you can use sandpaper to dull the very sharp X-acto blades before you use them. This protects both the fossil, in case you accidentally touch it, and *yourself*. Parents and mentors will love you for doing the sandpaper thing; they are usually squeamish about blood.

6. Clean off enough sediment so that you can see the general shape of the fossil.

7. Apply glue to any cracks. Be careful not to glue your fingers together, or your pants to your legs. Always put the cap back on the glue when you're not using it.

< 42 >

Use Good Techniques

Your first times in the field, you should not remove anything without your mentor watching, and you definitely should not remove anything large. Until you're an expert, *never* attempt to remove anything larger than, say, a zucchini. You could accidentally, permanently damage important fossils. Rely on your mentor, and report any amazingly amazing finds to your local museum or university. There is a good chance they will let you help excavate!

Okay, okay. But can you remove something small by yourself? Something easy? The answer depends on a couple of questions. First, is it a small bone next to a bunch of other bones? If so, *do not take it out!* Keep all parts of larger specimens together, and get help from professionals in those cases. Second, how stable is the little fossil you have your eye on? If it's something that can be collected safely, you might have found your first collecting project. Your main job is to *protect* it, prevent breaking, and pack it safely for travel so its secrets can be preserved.

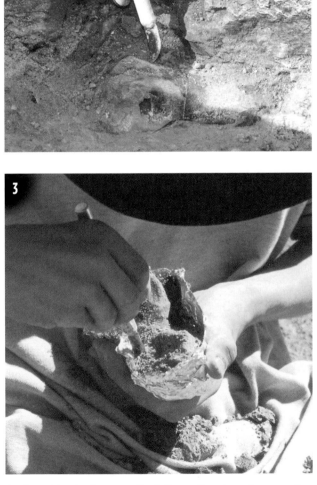

Graham Haydock correctly follows the steps in removing a fossil. Great job! (Terry Wentz)

This large block has several mushroom stems—you can see light through their tunnels *(inset)*. (The Toad)

For a small bone or fossil, simple techniques are fine. If you've glued the bone and it is sturdy, maybe all it will need is a piece of aluminum foil, some tape, and a label. If it is larger than that, you must determine if it should come out in one piece or several pieces. Is there a natural split already? Is this a good place to separate the fossil? If so, are loose fragments dangling? Be careful! Keep everything together! It's usually best to take out as large a piece as possible.

1. To prepare a fossil for removal, dig away the sediment from around its sides and bottom—until it looks like a mushroom, with the dirt as the stem and the fossil as the mushroom cap. Remember: this only

works if the fossil has been properly glued before the "mushrooming."

2. Cover the mushroom cap with aluminum foil, maybe a few pieces. Make sure to cover the dirt *under* the fossil—on the sides and bottom of the cap.

3. Tape around the edges, sides, and bottom of the fossil with strapping tape. Use the tape as support.

4. Once the cap is secure, firmly hold it with one hand (or have your mentor hold it) while you dig away the stem of dirt.

5. When the fossil comes off, turn it over and remove excess dirt. You may need to

< 44 >

After discovery, this fossil turtle is excavated, mushroomed, protected with foil and strapping tape, and covered with plaster and burlap for safe removal to the lab. (Layne Kennedy)

< 45 >

Heavy! (Layne Kennedy)

glue some cracks to keep the fossil together. Finish covering with foil. Finish taping.

6. Write on the tape what the fossil is, if you know, along with the date and location.

As you become more experienced, maybe by helping at museum or university digs, you'll learn more advanced techniques. You'll be able to help stabilize larger bones by putting layers of plaster-covered bandages over the foil. These are called *field jackets*. Extra-large bones or blocks of bones also need wooden splints, or even boards or steel, which can be plastered on. Removing these giant packages from the field requires much more than a backpack! I've moved some pretty big blocks, including one block that weighed more than nine thousand pounds!

Keeping Records

Fossils are cool, but they are only half the story. The other half is left behind in the rocks. That's why you have two important jobs: good collecting, and good record keeping. Any science you might do on a fossil depends on your paying attention to everything around the fossil and recording everything you can.

< 46 >

Mapping a fossil site is very important in understanding how a fossil got there. (Layne Kennedy)

Keeping records means:

1. Taking pictures—include something for scale, like a person, pen, ruler, or, in an emergency, a coin or hair scrunchie. Pictures should not only include close-ups of the fossil, but also panoramic views of the area, in case *National Geographic* has to find the spot again.

2. Drawing bone maps and recording sediment formations.

3. Writing standard information in your field notebook (see example on page 50). Keep in mind that it's important to record what you *do* see and what you *don't* see. If you've had a particularly bad day, with no fossils in sight, write that down so you don't go back there!

Whether or not you're good at drawing, you should make bone maps of all your sites. When you join a crew in the field, you will be very popular if you become a good map artist. Maps not only show how bones were arranged in the ground, but also give clues to how to put the bones back together. Or even why the fossil ended up this way—was it because of a river? Did scavengers move bones out of position? *Your map might even help you find missing bones!*

Every fossil is different. The more you dig, the more ideas you'll have to solve problems or mysteries. Maybe this saber-toothed cat is particularly fragile. Is there an extra-safe packaging solution? This *Triceratops* is on the edge of a cliff. How can I get a truck over there? I've never seen a fossil like this. Who can I bring to help me? These are the problems I love to solve. I bet you'll love them, too.

It's okay at first if you don't remember everything. But as you get more and more facts under your belt, it will be easier for you to know how important your fossil is. Is it one of a zillion sheep? Or the only "*Fabosaurus*" ever found? You'll know all about the area, the sediment, the age, the preservation, and what fossils were found with it. You'll know if scientists are arguing about this kind of fossil, or if it's really rather boring.

No matter what, though, your records will help. Especially if you really find "*Fabosaurus*," all the famous paleontologists in the whole wide world will want to read your notebook. Try to use good penmanship.

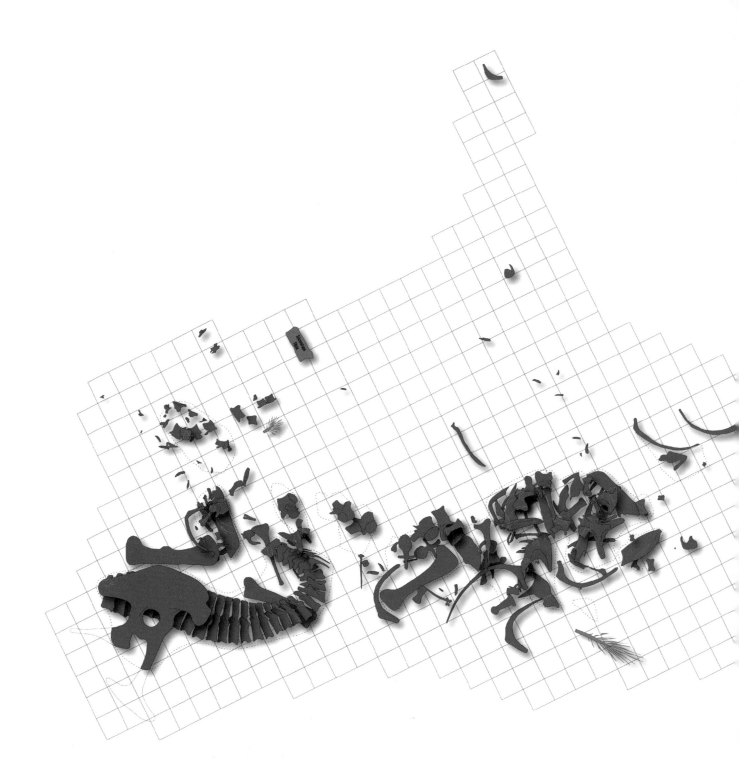

The map of the Stan *T. rex* site shows how the bones washed down an ancient riverbed. You can "see" the flow of the water by how the bones sprinkled away from the main carcass. (Peter Larson, Terry Wentz, Larry Shaffer, Matt Larson, Sam Farrar)

< 48 >

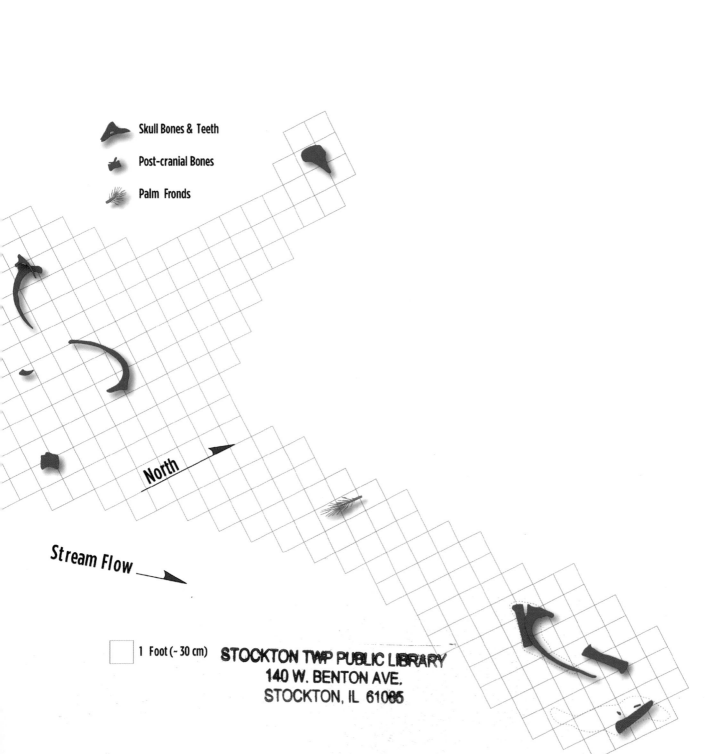

Skull Bones & Teeth

Post-cranial Bones

Palm Fronds

North

Stream Flow

1 Foot (~ 30 cm)

< 49 >

Sue's Field Record

Sue was the most excellent *T. rex* ever found—so far. Lots of people have asked to see my original notes from her dig site. Too bad I didn't write clearly so everyone could read them.

SPECIMEN NUMBER: SUE.8-14-90.MW This was the field number, and it forever recorded the date—August 14, 1990—and the location of Sue's site. The M and W were the initials of the landowner's name. Later, we added another number to Sue, BHI-3033, which was the catalog number in our museum.

SPECIMEN DESCRIPTION: *(At first I wrote)* Large *theropod*, or meat-eater's skeleton, some articulation in vertebral column. *(Later I added to this list, after we'd found more bones)* Left scapula-coracoid, humerus, cervical ribs, proximal end tibia, 2 femurs, pelvis, sacrum, 11 dorsal vertebrae, skull + lower jaw, ribs, metatarsal, 35 caudal vertebrae (8 without chevrons).

PRESERVATION: Good to excellent, some iron-stone concretions, some siltstone—mostly sand—comes away from bone well.

FORMATION: Approximately ten feet above base of lower Hell Creek Formation.

LOCATION: SE1/4, SW1/4, NW1/4, Sec. 32, T15N, R18E, Maurice Williams ranch, north east of Ruth Mason Quarry, Ziebach Co., South Dakota.

COLLECTOR: SUSAN HENDRICKSON, with Terry, Neal, Pete, Matthew, Jason.

CODE WORDS

Amber
Bone map
Cyanoacrylates
Field jacket
Frill

Global Positioning System (GPS)
Landowner
Mentor
Microsite

"Mushrooming"
Overburden
Polyvinyl acetate (PVA)
Sauropod
Theropod

< 50 >

Sue's Clues

How you'll collect a turtle that you can hold in your own two hands is exactly how we dig an entire thirty-foot-tall *Brachiosaurus* or a forty-foot-long *Tyrannosaurus rex*. Of course, we do it on a larger scale and use larger equipment, but the idea and general practice are the same.

Once you get the hang of digging out *one small* bone, you can dig out *lots* of bones. And *larger* bones. It's a matter of making sure you have enough people, enough of the right supplies and equipment, and enough knowledge.

Digging quarries where lots of bones are found together is exciting and fun. This is a big duckbill hadrosaur—named "Tadrosaur" because a guy named Tad found it. (The Toad)

< 51 >

Sue: What We Found and How We Found It . . . Well, *Her*

Sue's excavation is a perfect example of a challenging, rewarding dig site. For most of the dig, four of us did all the work—my brother and partner Neal, our wonderful digger and preparator Terry Wentz, the fossil's discoverer Susan Hendrickson, and me. At the beginning, my son Matt, who was ten, and my brother Neal's son Jason, fifteen, helped. Toward the end, our brother John and his pal Tater came to help move the huge bone blocks.

This is how it went: we first used picks to break up the rock, then we shoveled the chunks as far away as possible. Pick, shovel, throw. All day. Pick, shovel, throw. We could not reach Sue's steep dig site in our truck, or with any other vehicle. To create the gigantic shelf that would expose Sue's bones, we had to dig it by hand. No bulldozers. No earth movers. Not even a Bobcat.

Pick, shovel, throw. Another day, and another. And another.

Day after day for an entire week.

At first only Neal and I could fit on the shelf. Soon Terry and Susan could join us. Every night we returned to our nearby quarry camp completely exhausted, our skin caked with dirt, our muscles turned to rubber.

Before the digging had begun, we already had finished the first steps in our fossil excavation:

1. Picking up and labeling all the fragments on the ground.

2. Gluing any cracked bones sticking out of the hillside.

3. And then covering them with plaster and tarps.

Matt

Matt at age 10, with Susan Hendrickson and his *Triceratops.* (Peter Larson)

I know I'm a proud dad, but I'm not the only one who knows about Matt Larson. He was ten the year we dug Sue, and by then he was already an expert at finding fossils. He had been in the field with me his whole life, and from the time he was very small, I noticed he had an especially excellent "eye." He could see fossils from really far away, fossils that to almost anyone else would look like a chip of rock—or that wouldn't look like anything at all. A regular person wouldn't even *see* them.

Matt had the perfect combination of natural talent and experience. He would hang out at our dinosaur quarry each summer—a place where thousands of duckbills had been

We didn't want any rocks from above accidentally to fall or roll on the bones as we shoveled away the overburden. In this case, we had nearly thirty feet of rock above the fossil.

Pick, shovel, throw.

Finally we reached just above the bone layer, and Terry and Susan started digging with killed and tossed like salad. By the time he reached double digits, Matt could dig and remove bones all by himself.

But he also liked to go walking and looking, and he never seemed to get lost. He discovered plenty of fossils. That Sue Summer of 1990, he found a *Triceratops* skull. He knew what it was before he even touched it, because what he first saw was part of a horn sticking up. He dug on it for a while, checking its preservation and quality, before coming to get me.

As far as I know, Matt still holds the world's record for the number of *T. rex* teeth discovered in one season. He got very good at picking

Matt as a grown-up working on Bucky the *T. rex*. (The Toad)

The tooth that looks like a whole banana has its root; the other has been broken off. (Peter Larson)

out the color and texture of *shed* teeth, teeth that have been broken off. Shed teeth look like half a banana instead of a whole one. When you find a tooth with its root, it means the dinosaur died with the tooth in its mouth—and when the gums rotted, it fell out. When you find a shed tooth, someone was eating or fighting nearby—and snapped that tooth right off!

Every time we turned around that summer, Matt was showing us another shed tooth. He found twenty-one! Now Matt is twenty-four years old, and he runs our volunteer digs each summer—teaching kids and adults who come to visit. He has a t-shirt that says, "Your dream is my day job." He *dares you* to beat his record!

knives, while Neal and I kept shoveling away.

Susan uncovered ribs, while Terry dazzled us by finding the ilium, a five-foot-long and nearly three-foot-wide hip bone. He also began uncovering the articulated *dorsal* vertebrae, Sue's backbone, that Susan had first seen poking from the cliff. Finally Neal and I could join in the

most fun part of the digging process: *looking for bones!* It was like a giant treasure hunt.

Within two days, we could see enough of the right side of Sue's magnificent skull to know what it was. Her head stretched out to five feet long, was nearly three feet wide—maybe bigger than you!—and her nose was pinned under her

Above: You can see Neal on the skinny shelf, waving his shovel in the air. (Peter Larson) *Left:* Terry illustrates the "throw" part of pick, shovel, throw. (Susan Hendrickson)

pelvis. Even through the jumble, her face looked perfect. We could see lots of bumpy ridges and textured areas, and plenty of teeth sticking out. What a smile!

After another week, Sue's gigantic frame surrounded us, and we felt very small. Instead of getting all freaked out by how amazing she was, we just worked to uncover more. Each knife blade delicately found the layer between bone and earth. We lay on our sides on the rocky ground, or balanced on our knees and elbows for entire days, faces within inches of the earth, watching for any sign of bone. Our hands moved like machines. We shot the thin secret-sauce superglue into hairline cracks, knowing it would instantly slip down the tiniest tunnels, bonding splinters back into place. We used our softest brushes to sweep away dusty debris so we could check for a color or texture that might be bone—the smallest bits of something important could be lost forever if they fell into a crack.

We were having so much fun that the only

< 54 >

Susan and Sue, when one of them was still partially stuck in the sediment. (Peter Larson)

Working within Sue's coiled skeleton. (Peter Larson)

< 55 >

Nighttime in the field is when we record all the details from the day's work, such as cataloguing bones. (BHI file photo)

way we realized hours had passed was when our necks cramped or the sun set. Each motion of our hands revealed something new. It was a magical time, as if we were Sue's doctors, carefully bringing her back to life. It was impossible to even think about stopping until we lost the light of the sun each evening.

Each day, we kept digging, gluing, wrapping, mapping, and removing bone after bone. Finally we had only the really big stuff left.

We began by mushrooming the bones four to ten inches above the ground. The larger the bone, the higher the stem. We glued or PVA'd exposed fractures, layered on heavy-duty aluminum foil and strapping tape. These bones or

blocks were big enough that we couldn't stop there: we mixed plaster of paris and water into a watery paste.

Over and over, mushroom, glue, foil, tape, plaster. We took turns dragging strips of gauze and then burlap bandages through the white paste, creating the plaster covers called jackets. If the bone was very large, we added splints of wood held in place with more bandages, and ended with a straight layer of plaster mixed with water.

After the casts hardened, we turned them over, cleaned their undersides, glued some more, and wrote field number and bone name on the jackets with a marker. After all of the

< 56 >

Large plaster jackets are sometimes engineering feats. (Susan Hendrickson)

single bones and small groups of bones had been removed, we were left with one huge mass—a bunch of intertwined body parts difficult to separate in the field. This is the type of block that some lucky scientists have removed with a helicopter.

Of course, we didn't have a helicopter. Even with this giant block, we did the same procedure—except we made it into one enormous mushroom, two feet above the ground, supported on four stems. As we worked, we found a few *fissures,* places where the block would naturally fracture apart, which was great. We gently allowed the pieces to come apart before we plastered and removed them. In the end, the biggest

section was eight feet wide, eleven feet long, and nearly three feet thick. This is like having four single beds in a square—two wide and two long. Imagine how heavy that much rock would be! We later learned it weighed about 9,000 pounds. That's as much as a school bus full of all your pals!

In order to move the block, we screwed a wooden frame together around and under it. Using levers and cables attached to the frame, we pulled and slid the block onto a truck bed. While slow and difficult, and at times scary, this method was similar to how the Egyptians moved those huge blocks for the pyramids—except they didn't have trucks!

< 57 >

Bars and winches—and physics!—were used to move Sue's largest blocks. (Susan Hendrickson)

What It All Means

Digging out Sue took nearly one thousand work hours. For one person, that would be forty-two days non-stop, 24/7—with no sleep. With the number of people we had, and the experience we had, we were able to do it in seventeen days. It took people and tools and machines and geometry and math and physics.

But getting the bones safely from the sediment and into the truck is only half of what happens in the field.

We started by checking off the list of the bones we were seeing. Check: the best *T. rex* shoulder blades ever found—54 inches long. Check: only the second *T. rex* arm and hand ever found (her

right one). Check: backbone. Check: her amazing skull. Check: Sue's left hind leg, articulated together but yanked from its socket in the pelvis and drifted downstream a few feet.

But wait a minute!

My brother Neal noticed it first. At least two-thirds of the fibula, the smaller of the two lower leg bones, was all fat and bumpy. This was *exostosis*, a growth of extra bone that happens when a bone is broken or infected and tries to heal. When we looked closer, we could see where the break started.

Any digger would be interested in the *fact* that the bone was messed up. But a paleontologist with a good imagination wonders what that fact might mean. I started to think about it. Had

< 58 >

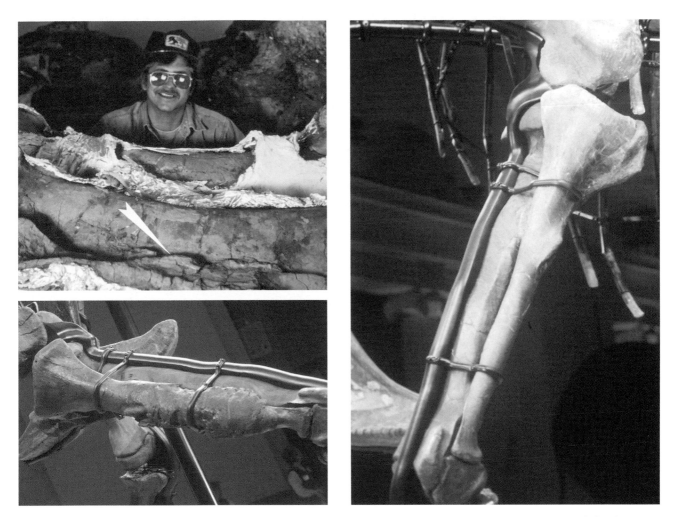

Top left: Neal with Sue's lower left leg, showing what he first noticed—Sue's broken bone. (Ed Gerken) *Bottom left:* The same bone after cleaning and mounting. Notice the swollen shaft. (Peter Larson) *Right:* Compare Sue's damaged left leg with this undamaged right leg. Can you see the difference? (Peter Larson)

she broken her leg skiing? Not likely. Maybe she slipped and fell, or was whacked in the leg by the tail club of an ankylosaur.

When a person breaks a leg, it's a big deal. People walk on two legs. Sue walked on two legs. I figured it would be a *huge deal* if I chased and killed and ate what amounts to 1,200 hamburgers in one sitting—every day—and suddenly I couldn't *run!* How did she live? Did she have help? I imagined Sue's husband or daughter delivering dinner: "You want fries with that? Would you like it *supersized?*"

It's important to mention that not all paleontologists agree with us about the broken-ness of Sue's leg. Everyone agrees that *something* happened to it, but some people think the injury might not have been bad enough to keep Sue bed-ridden. A closer look at that bone may provide the answer.

The leg problem wasn't Sue's only *pathology,* or scar from an injury. We found so many scars that we figured she had been the heavyweight kick-boxing champion of the world. We started looking for her trophy.

< 59 >

Sue's broken and partially healed ribs. (Peter Larson)

This is what it means to be a thorough paleontologist. As you're digging, you're gathering clues not just about a dinosaur's death, but also its life. At one time or another, Sue suffered from many broken and sometimes infected ribs, crushed tail vertebrae, a torn tendon on the right upper arm, and multiple injuries to the head—not to mention the badly broken lower leg. We could tell by looking at the bones that all of these injuries had healed, or at least begun to heal. *So what did we know about Sue?*

1. There was no way all of these injuries could have happened during the same heated argument! If all of those parts had been broken at once, Sue would have died.

2. To me, this said that plenty of time passed between one rough encounter and the next.

3. It might take months for one of those awful injuries to heal, and Sue needed to be fully healthy and strong to survive the next one. That requires plenty of time to heal between injuries—so she was probably pretty old when she died.

4. And if she had a lifetime of rough encounters, ouch! It doesn't sound very fun to have been a *T. rex*.

5. She was gnarly.

< 60 >

Mystery: Old Age

How can we tell how old a dinosaur was when it died? There is no exact, scientific method that can tell for sure. Scientists have tried counting "rest lines" and "growth rings" in bones. These lines in some cases represent growth spurts. Unfortunately, unlike in a tree, or even in animals we can observe alive, we have no idea whether each line represented a year or a season.

Until we find better clues to unlock this mystery, we can rely only on the models we see in animals today—and on guesses. We know that large animals usually have longer lives than small ones. Many can live for 60 years or even longer—animals like elephants, crocodiles, and some birds, especially macaws and eagles. The all-time record-holders: turtles. Some of them have been documented to be more than 200 years old!

So how old was Sue? To have lived through so many injuries, we can guess that she walked the earth, oh, maybe 60 years? Maybe 80? Maybe even 100!

Boys and Girls

Getting to know your fossil personally is the whole reason to go collecting. Sue was a friend of the family right away, and this was especially easy because I named her Sue. At first, the name came from the amateur collector who discovered her, Susan Hendrickson. But after a while, Sue was like a person with her own personality.

That's when we started to wonder: "What if we're calling this dinosaur a girl's name, and she's a boy?" Since she was bigger than any other *T. rex* ever found, some people thought she was a boy. Aren't boys always bigger? Or did the world's scariest monster wear a dress?

I decided to start a research project on the spot. It would take a long time to develop my hypothesis and to test it, because a lot of Sue's bones were hiding in the blocks. I started in the library, and then I looked at living creatures and other *T. rex* skeletons.

I found out a few things:

1. Just like in people, there are two sizes of *T. rex*: a big, tough, beefy one, and a smaller, more delicate one. Scientists call them *robust* and *gracile*.

2. Those knobby "eyebrows" on the skull

< 61 >

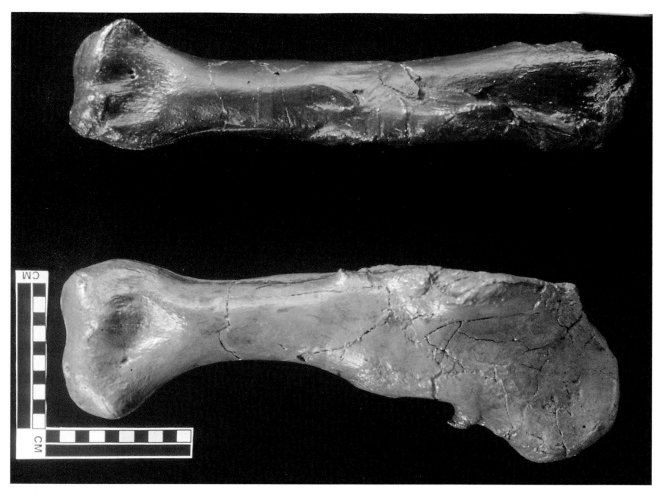

These two arms could show differences in dinosaur gender . . . but which is which? (Peter Larson)

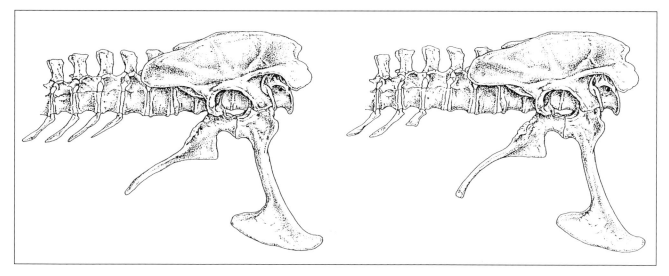

There are two different types of *T. rex* skeletons with different pelves and chevrons (spines below the tail). The robust form (right) has more room for the passage of eggs. (Dorothy Sigler Norton)

< 62 >

Ken Carpenter, the first to think the biggest, baddest *T. rex* might be female. (Courtesy of Ken Carpenter)

This male bison has to throw his weight around to be the boss of his herd. (Layne Kennedy)

are different in the two types. Other bones also are different, such as the upper arm bone, called the humerus. In the robust type, it is not only bigger, but also curved.

3. My pal Ken Carpenter at the Denver Museum of Nature and Science had noticed that the robust type had more up-and-down room in the pelvis. He wondered if this was for laying eggs. Since Ken is a paleontological genius, I figured that I should pay close attention. "He could be right," I thought.

4. In insects, clams, snails, crustaceans, fishes, turtles, snakes, and some birds, *girls are bigger than boys*. Most people *think* that boys are always bigger, because they are in people and in some of the animals we know best, like cattle, sheep, and dogs. It's also true for primates: us—and our closest relatives, monkeys and apes. It's *not* true for hyenas and some whales—the biggest animal *ever* is the *female* blue whale.

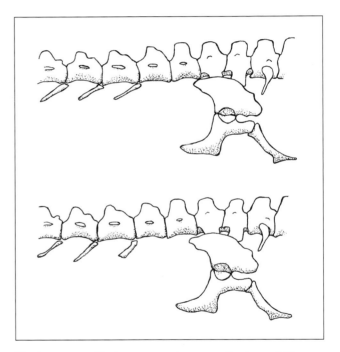

The boy crocodile bones are shown on the top; girl bones on the bottom. (Peter Larson)

5. Bigger boys are usually the case when the males of a species fight for a mate. In creatures where no fighting is necessary, girls are usually larger. They need room to carry their eggs or develop babies. Boys don't need this extra body size.

Sue at the Field Museum. (Peter Larson)

6. Living boy crocodiles—the closest living thing resembling *T. rex* ancestors—have a special bone under their tail that hooks to their sex organs. It's called a chevron. Girl crocodiles don't need a bone like that, so theirs is very small and points out of the way. (Girls and boys have other chevrons, not just the one we're talking about.)

7. Not all of the other *T. rex* that had been found had their under-the-tail parts preserved. The ones that did seemed to have this same tail bone arrangement. Girls with a small bone, boys with a bigger one!

I decided that if Sue had the "girl" tail bone, I had good evidence for a theory. It took several years for her preparation to be fully completed by Chicago's Field Museum, which became her permanent home. When I was finally able to see her finished tail area, here's what I saw:

- Sue DOES have the "girl" tail bone!

- Sue's pelvis is not only "taller," but also wider than a gracile *T. rex*'s. This could be important for laying eggs.

- Sue has a pathology on the top side of her tail—several bones are injured and healed, even almost linking together because of an injury. I think this injury might be due to how *T. rex* had to mate! The male would have rested on her tail, and he would have been *very heavy!*

< 64 >

Sue's chevrons show that if she was anything like a crocodile, she was a girl. (Peter Larson)

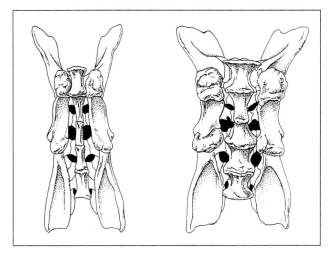

Sue's pelvis, when seen from below (right), was much wider than the gracile form. (Dorothy Sigler Norton)

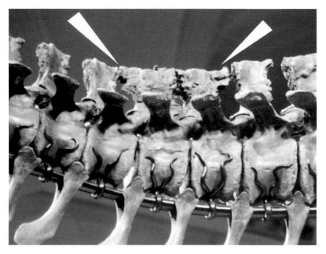

The pathology on top of Sue's tail. (Peter Larson)

< 65 >

I think Sue is a girl! More research over the coming years will prove if my theory is right. If it is, the biggest and baddest *T. rex* were females. My same gender theory seems to hold true for other meat-eating dinosaurs (remember: *theropods*). However, this doesn't mean scientists have made big conclusions about the sex of other types of dinosaurs! There is lots of research to be done—maybe you can help us?

Kids

Where I live, in South Dakota, *T. rex* fossils are found in the Hell Creek Formation. The sediments were deposited pretty slowly, and most dinosaurs were eaten or kicked around before they could be preserved. They are very incomplete, or easily crumble into bits, or are mostly washed away by the time we find them. Plus there's another danger: *sinkholes!*

Hell Creek sinkholes developed from underground water flowing into cracks in the sediment of a hill. As rains added more water, the holes expanded, pulling earth and bones and rocks sometimes five feet, sometimes thirty, sometimes hundreds of feet down! The third *T. rex* I dug with my company was a male named Duffy—and we found some of his parts right next to a sinkhole.

The dig was very hard, because Duffy's bones were all spread out. We weren't sure if most of him had been sucked down the hole, or if he had washed away from the site. It was very frustrating. It also rained a lot during that dig, and the sediment was super-gooey and muddy. When we walked anywhere, our shoes collected huge globs of mud. We were all walking on plat-

"See any bones down there, Pete?" (BHI file photo)

form shoes, sometimes six inches off the ground, and our feet were sooooo heavy.

It was on an icky day, when everyone was crabby, that we realized something fantastic. Slowly but surely, we had already uncovered, mapped, and removed twenty-five nicely preserved, although broken, bones—including at least ten ribs, a half-dozen vertebrae, and weirdly broken and scattered chunks of a bone from the pelvis. Then we realized there was something amazing going on here.

Only two *T. rex* had ever been found with their complete *scapula-coracoids*—the double-

< 66 >

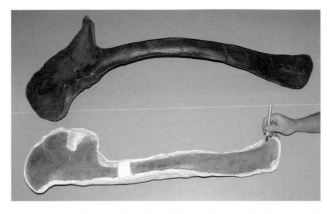

You can see that Duffy's shoulder girdle, on the bottom, is smaller than the adult's above. (Peter Larson)

Ontogeny! From little kid to adolescent to big teenager, Paleo Pete's face changes right before our eyes! (Family photos)

boned shoulder structures. Not only did our Duffy have both sets, right and left, but also they were strangely small. Sue's, the biggest, were fifty-four inches long. Duffy's were only thirty-six inches.

Approximately 75 percent grown, Duffy represented the equivalent of a thirteen-year-old person! Right there in the middle of our crabbiness, we got all excited thinking about *ontogeny*, how a creature grows and changes in its lifetime. Our wave of enthusiasm didn't last long, though. Long ago the terrible sinkhole might have gobbled up two-thirds of Duffy. I think it ate most of our first teenage dinosaur.

But that's okay. Duffy was an ontogeny starting point. One lonely teenager isn't enough when it comes to meaningful scientific observation. We need to have a look at more teenagers—and, for that matter, kids of all ages—to even have a clue what the questions are.

Luckily, there are more. Bucky and Black Beauty (see next page for her story) are both teenagers. Tinker and LACM 23845, a specimen from the Los Angeles County Museum, are like eleven-year-olds. When we compare all of these kids, we can see the beginnings of a hypothesis.

< 67 >

Black Beauty

Black Beauty is one of the best *T. rex* ever found. She was poking out of a riverbank in southwestern Alberta, Canada, and Jeff Baker found her. A teenaged high school student at the time, he had been fishing with no luck. It's a good thing he was better at spotting bones than catching fish.

It was the summer of 1980, and it was hot, and the fish weren't biting, and Jeff took a walk. He saw something black in the light gray sandstone of the bank, maybe thirty feet up. When he scrambled up there, he poked at it for about an hour before going to find his friend and fishing buddy, Brad Mercier. They returned the next day with yet another pal from school, and together the guys chiseled out a few boxes of bones.

Of course, they showed everything to their teachers, who sent the boys directly to the nearest paleontologist, Dr. Phil Currie. Currie's team began excavation in 1982, and all kinds of challenges made the dig interesting. The rock was really hard, the sediment covering the specimen was thick—they needed a bulldozer to remove it—and a nearby freight train spilled poisonous gases

Black Beauty, the first *T. rex* found by a teenager, has a great skull. (Peter Larson)

and forced everyone to evacuate. You see? Paleontologists simply won't give up.

Black Beauty's best parts are her skull and those long legs. However, while plenty of her backbone and hip vertebrae were recovered, no tail! Currie thinks it may still be in the cliff, and he plans to hunt for it one day.

Why the name Black Beauty? Because the mineral manganese filtered into the bones from the underground water, dying the skeleton jet black. Lots of *T. rex* are dark brown, but she's the only black one.

Duffy had big eyes, and a huge mouth with huge teeth—all oversized and out of proportion. In living mammals—even people—we're used to seeing big eyes in babies. Try comparing current photos of your parents or other adults you know with photos when they were little kids. You'll see that their kid-heads, kid-faces, and kid-eyes were larger in proportion on their little bodies than

their grown-up features are on their grown-up bodies.

That's how Duffy looks, too. But we were surprised about the long muzzle. Usually, puppies—and baby duckbills—have short, cute noses to go with their big eyes. This huge *T. rex* snout was unusual—and scary.

If you have older sisters or brothers, you may

< 68 >

Long and spindly legs are often the mark of a youngster.
(Katherine Kuhn, iStockphoto)

the ground right now, an eleven-year-old and a teenager. I can't wait to get my tape measure out! Meanwhile, for more information, I've been comparing living animals to my collection of kids—and not just their snouts.

In running animals, like deer and horses, legs grow quickly so babies can scamper very soon after being born. Just like them, Black Beauty and another, fragmentary specimen have long, skinny leg bones. Plus, Bucky's toes and LACM's feet are huge for their body sizes. Okay, now I'm seeing three-foot-long, enthusiastic, wide-eyed, big-mouthed, long-legged, big-footed, adorable killing machines.

Despite my imagination, though, we simply don't have enough information yet to form a theory. All we can say is: the *preliminary evidence* suggests that these creatures *might* have grown in stages similar to animals we know today. Keep your eyes open for more youngsters—in lots of dinosaur species. Like puppies, did they have floppy feet? Like foals, did they have long, gangly legs? Like Charlie Brown, did they have big heads?

What else can kid fossils tell us, aside from how their species grew?

For fun, I compared the skeletons to see if there were gender differences in youth. Bucky's two shoulder blades are significantly more robust than Duffy's—and you already know that I think the robust *T. rex* are girls. And Tinker's robust upper arm bone is curved, also like a girl's. So once we get more sure of ourselves, Bucky and Tinker may be in for some name changes.

Okay, anything else? YES. Kids can tell us something about *families*.

I'll never forget the moment, while digging up

have noticed that when they reach the Terrible Teenage period, they get weird growth spurts. Their bones start to move around, and their faces actually change shape. Ack. Not to mention their *moods*. Ack! Maybe that explains Duffy's long, gnarly snout. Perhaps he was in the middle of a growth spurt. *I'm glad I didn't meet him in person*, a morphing, acky teenager with HUGE TEETH.

As we continue to find *T. rex* in all sizes, we can start to "map" their growth and "watch" their bodies change. I'm looking forward to meeting two new kids who are coming out of

< 69 >

See my hand? I'm holding the eight-year-old's lacrimal (the bone in front of the eye) next to Sue's giant one. (Ed Gerken)

< 70 >

Mystery: Missing Children

Why are so few young *T. rex* discovered? If kids grew quickly, not much time would pass before they were as big as their parents. Some of you might *already* be as tall as your parents. (We parents hate that!) For paleontologists, this means that there would be only a short time to "catch" and preserve *T. rex* youngsters in sediment before they grew to adult size.

Also, while they were small, most likely kids were tasty treats for bigger beasts. Maybe not very many of them made it to the sediment!

Another idea to keep in mind: *fratricide*, which means "killing your brother." In some animals, such as birds of prey, sometimes the strongest babies will kill—and even eat—their weaker siblings. Yikes! No wonder we find more big ones!

Paleo Pete hopes his brother Neal doesn't get any funny ideas about fratricide!

Sue's grave, when I realized *she was not alone.* In the field, we found parts of another adult buried with her. He was smaller than Sue. Also, there were skull pieces from an eight-year-old equivalent and a baby. Other dinosaur sites have revealed the same thing: more than one creature in the same hole.

So, we have dinner being served to a *T. rex* in the hospital with a broken leg, and we have several *T. rex* living in the same "house." While we cannot be sure yet, it seems as if evidence is piling up to suggest that *T. rex* was a creature who lived with its family.

CODE WORDS

Chevron	Pathology
Dorsal	Primates
Exostosis	Robust
Fissures	Rooted tooth
Fratricide	Shed tooth
Gender	Siblings
Gracile	Sinkhole
Ontogeny	

Above: A fossil turtle in the wild.
(Layne Kennedy)

Left: A fossil turtle in captivity.
(Layne Kennedy)

What to Do with Your Fossil
Once You Get It Home

I know, I know, you worked so hard out in the field. It was hot, and mosquitoes sucked you dry and the prickle-burrs poked through your socks. You spotted that turtle and you nearly twisted your ankle hopping that gully to get to it. But it's a beautiful turtle. And it's your turtle. Your mentor helped you carefully collect it, the landowner let you keep it, and now you think your work is done.

Wrong.

Here's some math for you: a fossil that took only one hour to collect may easily take ten, one hundred, or one thousand hours to clean, restore, and get ready for exhibit.

1 hour's collecting = **10 hours** or **100 hours** or even **1,000 hours** of preparing!

You probably go to school about seven hours a day. With lunch and recess and breaks between classes, you're actually sitting in your chair for between five and six hours.

1,000 preparing hours ÷ 5.5 hours in a school day = 181.82 school days.

If you dug up a very delicate, dainty, broken-to-bits, fabulous little fossil, it might take you one hundred eighty-two school days—most of the year—to prepare it. Guess how long it takes to prepare a *T. rex*?

I'll tell you later. We have more important fish to fry, or turtles to toast, or . . . .

I know you're asking, "Should I just give up now?" Of course not! You just need to learn about *preparation*, the process of cleaning and preserving a fossil. Some paleontologists think this is the best part, because a fossil goes from a dirty, crusty old thing into a shiny, wonderful old thing. Once you know how to do preparation work, six months will fly by before you know it. (Besides, don't forget: it might only take ten hours, or one hundred hours—which equals only nineteen days.)

< 73 >

One lovely, shiny theropod toe bone
after cleaning. (Layne Kennedy)

Teeth, before and after cleaning. (Layne Kennedy)

< 74 >

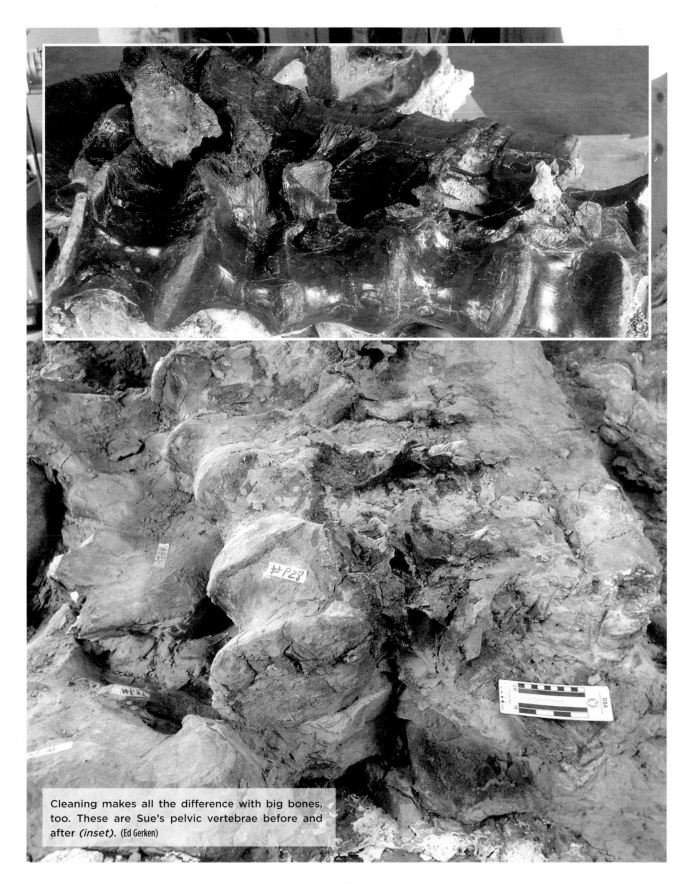

Cleaning makes all the difference with big bones, too. These are Sue's pelvic vertebrae before and after *(inset).* (Ed Gerken)

< 75 >

The Paleo Laboratory: Training to Clean Fossils

Just like in collecting fossils, there are different levels of being a preparator. Some of the work you can do at home, but some can only happen in a laboratory with lots of fancy equipment. Once you become best friends with preparators in your local museum or university, you'll be able to watch and learn every step in the fossil beauty school. However, please note! Just like with Dad, never borrow a preparator's tools without asking!

At first, before going at your splendiferous turtle, it might be a good idea to practice on some scraps of bone that are not as cool. You probably saw plenty to choose from on your walkabout. Here's what you'll need:

Prep Kit	Expert Kit
Paintbrushes	Paintbrushes
Toothbrushes	Toothbrushes
X-acto knives (with extra blades)	X-acto knives

WARNING: these are very sharp!

Prep Kit	Expert Kit
Scribes (like dental tools)	Sharp-point scribe, flat / rounded-tip scribe
Elmer's Glue & Superglue	Superglue & Epoxy
PVA	PVA
Hammer	Hammers
Chisels & punches (pointy chisels)	Chisels & punches (pointy chisels)
Metric tape measure	Metric tape measure
Lab notebook	Lab notebook
Pen & Pencil	Pen & Pencil
	Knife
	Acetone
	Medium-stiff brush
	Nippers
	Awls
	Needles
	Pin vices
	Flexible shaft tool
	Air scribe / compressor
	Air brade / baking soda
	Air grinder
	Ultraviolet light
	Binocular microscope
	CAT scanner

This is the basic stuff you'll need to get started. (Peter Larson)

< 76 >

Sometimes a big bone block makes a good museum exhibit. In this case, the bones of this duckbill were never removed from the matrix. (Layne Kennedy)

< 77 >

Mystery: Dirty Words

Fossil dirt: I know we've spent two chapters calling the dirt "sediment," but now we're going to call it something else. There's actually a good reason. Instead of thinking of big layers of dirt deposited over large areas—sediment—we're going to think of smaller areas of dirt.

When dirt is only something surrounding a fossil, it's called *matrix*.

General dirt: Just for the record, "dirt" usually means *soil*, the topmost layer of the earth where plants grow. Dirt can be *sand*, *silt* (very fine), or *clay* (very, very fine). Ancient dirt, or soil, becomes rock. This doesn't necessarily mean it gets hard. Sandstone, siltstone and even claystone may be as loose as the day it was deposited—or, it may be, well, hard as a rock.

Once we get a dinosaur settled in the laboratory, working on it at first is almost like our original outdoor digging process. Except for the sun and mosquitoes and burrs. We have to slowly uncover each bone and untangle it from the others. Then, we clean each bone separately. This is no different from what you will do. In a professional laboratory, all the skills you're learning are just done in bigger quantities and with bigger tools. You can do this.

Every move you make in preparation is permanent, so if you get very close to the bone and get nervous, stop! Ask your mentor what to do next. Meanwhile, here are the basic steps:

1. Continue the process you started in the field—gently remove matrix from the fossil, starting as far away from the bone as possible.

2. Use smaller and smaller knives or dental tools the closer you get to the bone.

3. Hold a knife with the blade pointing away from you and toward the fossil, pushing or pulling it gently to free bits of matrix. The idea is for the matrix to let go without the knife's pointy parts touching the bone. (When using an X-acto knife, remember to dull the blade with sandpaper!)

4. Glue any cracks in the bone as you uncover them.

5. If any of your old glue from the field needs to be removed, try the X-acto knife or small dental picks to peel it away. Remember, no *scraping*, no touching the bone with the sharp part of the blade!

6. Watch for anything scientific. Like some little creature trapped behind your turtle's leg, or anything weird about the matrix—record it in your notebook.

< 78 >

Mystery: How Careful Do You Really Have to Be?

To successfully remove matrix from your turtle, you focus on the rock surface—not the fossil's surface. Except in the final stages of cleaning—with proper technique, extreme caution, and plenty of careful instruction—no tool except a soft brush should touch the turtle itself. How important is this rule? On a scale of 1 to 10, where 1 is the hardness of baby powder and 10 the hardness of diamond, bone has a hardness of about 3.5, and your tooth enamel is about 4.5. Either your teeth or steel—which has a hardness from 5 to 7—will always scratch bone if you poke it hard enough. Please note! *Never* use your mom's diamond ring to clean fossils! It will hurt the fossils, and your mom will hurt you.

Knowing the hardness of your tools will help prevent mistakes and injuries to fossils while you're cleaning them. (Peter Larson)

Hardness	1	1.5	2	2.5	3	3.5	4	4.5	5
Item or tool	talc(soft)	baking soda	brush/fingernail			bone		teeth	steel/knife

5.5	6	6.5	7	7.7	8	8.5	9	9.5	10
glass	chisel/X-acto		file			grinder			diamond (hard)

< 79 >

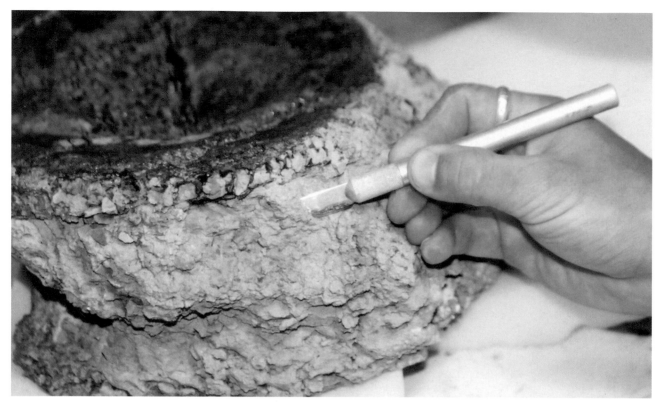

Knife position is crucial! Never aim the sharp end at the fossil. (Peter Larson)

A little goes a long way when it comes to superglue. (Peter Larson)

< 80 >

Sandy Gerken knows the right way to use tools; here she's using a scribe for final cleaning of a bunch of turtles—they're nicknamed Snow White and the Seven Dwarves. (Layne Kennedy)

< 81 >

What does it mean when you find bits of turtle stuck between the teeth of a *Camarasaurus*? Since *Camarasaurus* was a plant eater, there must be some other explanation besides dinner. (Peter Larson)

7. When you're *very close* to the bone and there's only a thin layer of matrix left, go slowly! With your very smallest tool, gently try to push or pull the tool across the matrix, *charming* the rock from the bone—just ask it nicely to let go.

8. Apply PVA when you're done.

In a laboratory, you'll see a fantastic tool that saves a lot of time in fossil cleaning. This is an *air scribe*, which looks like a metal pencil hooked by a tube to an air compressor. Air scribes act like miniature chisels because the air pushes the tip up and down, faster than you can see it go.

The hardened tip chips away at teeny pieces of matrix. It's important to have many hours of preparation behind you when you first grab one of these, because they can blast away the fossil just as easily as the matrix!

You'll also see preparators in the laboratory wearing magnifying glasses or looking through a microscope as they work with tweezers and very tiny-tipped scribes, like your dentist's tooth-cleaning tool. This is a very special skill, and you may have it if you're hands don't shake

< 82 >

A final coat of PVA helps protect the surface of the fossil from oils and dirt found on the probing fingers of paleontologists. (BHI file photo)

< 83 >

Terry using an air scribe to remove pyrite, a very hard iron mineral, from an *Acrocanthosaurus*. (Layne Kennedy)

< 84 >

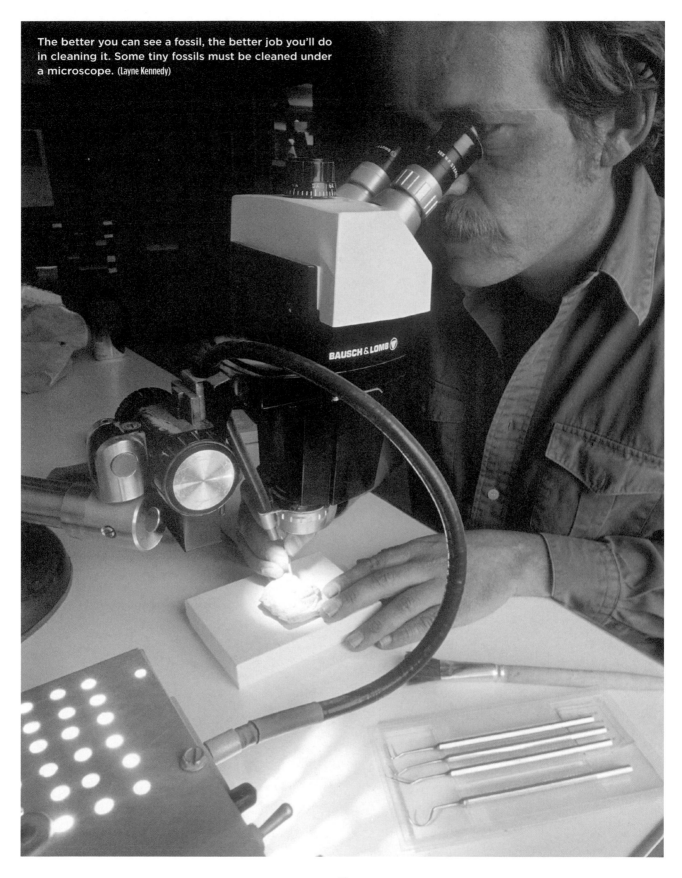

The better you can see a fossil, the better job you'll do in cleaning it. Some tiny fossils must be cleaned under a microscope. (Layne Kennedy)

< 85 >

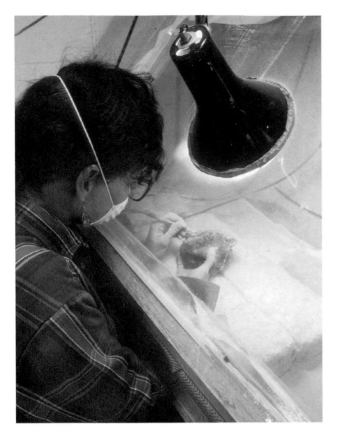

(some people are shakier than others), if you're especially good at puzzles, and if you're very patient.

Finally, bone can be cleaned down to the level you can see with a microscope. For this there are two choices. One is the *air brade*. This tool is used inside a small version of a sandblasting cabinet—like a big box with a window in front and holes for your hands. Instead of blasting grains of sand, we use baking soda. Its hardness is only 1.5, which means it's like giving the fossil a gentle, delicate bath. When this process is finished, even a giant *T. rex* will gleam.

Another way to clean tiny spaces is with chemicals. Paleontologists with good knowledge of chemistry work with acids that dissolve matrix but don't hurt bones. If you've been kicked out of science class for creating explosions, this might be your specialty.

Shirley Duwenhoegger uses an air brade for final cleaning. (Ed Gerken)

< 86 >

Filling in the Gaps

Fossils are never perfect. After you'd been buried under hundreds of feet of heavy sediment, how would you feel? Smushed and bumped and crushed out of shape with some of your parts missing.

After you've cleaned your turtle within an inch of its life, there's a very good chance that something will be missing. Maybe there are cracks in it, or a chunk that was washed away before you found it—or even something you accidentally threw away. Now is the time for art class.

There are two basic skills that come with *reconstruction*, or making missing parts. One is carefully applying putty into cracks—and then dabbing it with wrinkled paper, a brush, or scratching the surface with a pin so that it matches the real fossil's texture. The other is creating totally

A *T. rex* ilium before restoration *(top)* and after *(bottom)*. (Neal Larson)

< 87 >

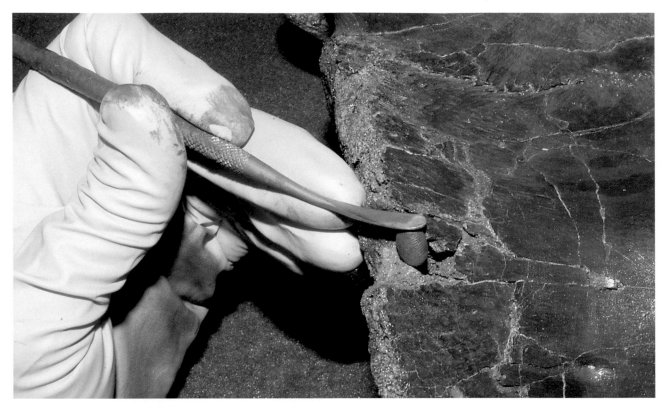

Epoxy putty works well for filling small cracks. (Peter Larson)

Look closely at the edge of this turtle shell. Shirley has done major restoration with epoxy putty. Can you see what is real and what is made? (Ed Gerken)

< 88 >

missing parts, using sculpture. If your turtle is missing a piece of its shell, you make a fake one by copying another section of shell.

I like to use two-part epoxy putty. When the parts are combined, the stuff feels like clay. Once it's "set," it's durable and strong, but still can be removed if you made a mistake. To remove putty, you can either soften it with heat—a hair dryer works well—or air brade it away when it's dry. If you're having trouble finding epoxy putty, try the plumbing department in your hardware store.

For really large areas or missing bones like a *T. rex* femur, instead you could use a water-

Mystery: Fluorescence

Researchers can double-check to see what's restored. Next time you go to a mineral and crystal exhibit in a museum, visit the "fluorescent room." There, in the dark, minerals *fluoresce*, or glow with bright colors under ultraviolet or infrared light. Fossil restoration can be detected by using this process, because there are minerals in most fossils.

The point of shining ultraviolet or infrared lights at *minerals* is to see the rock in a different way. Maybe it's a gray rock, and you want to be positively sure which gray rock it is. Since minerals react to ultraviolet and infrared lights differently than to the light we usually see, these gray minerals might suddenly "glow" pink or blue or yellow. Once we know which rocks make which colors, we can easily identify them. Fluorescence also looks cool.

The point of shining ultraviolet or infrared lights at *fossils* is to be able to "see" the minerals in them. Putty and paint have different chemicals than real bones, so usually the fake parts don't bounce back colors. They're just dark. Not only can these special lights reveal restoration, but also they might show details hidden to the naked eye—like antennae, feathers, skin, or even guts.

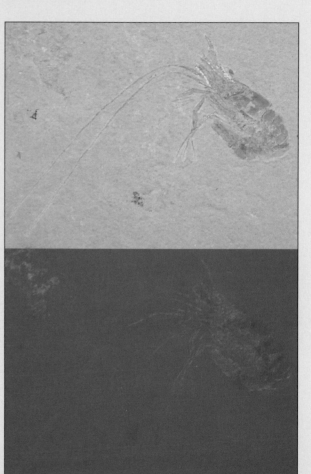

Compare this shrimp from Lebanon under natural light *(top)* and ultraviolet light *(bottom)*. In the bottom frame, you can see painted restoration—dark blobs in the body—and otherwise invisible extra-fine legs. (Peter Larson)

< 89 >

Mystery: Putting It Together

Many paleontologists *dig* fossils, and *prepare* fossils, but they often don't make their own casts or build the actual museum displays. This is because making molds and welding steel are very different skills than usual paleontology skills like finding and digging and scraping and measuring and comparing and imagining.

However, for me, when I actually use my own hands to put the bones together—feeling how an animal stood in its life—I learn how that animal moved. That's why I wanted to know how to bend and shape metal, and how to put parts together. I enjoy thinking about everything from how to attach a rib, to how to wheel a whole long-neck—in parts—through a "people door."

Ken Carpenter, my friend at the Denver Museum of Nature and Science, is great at this. He'll tell you that no matter what you *think* about how a leg fits in a joint, or how a tail moves, you don't really *know* until you try to string the bones together. Try it sometime, with your warrior robot toys that have interchangeable parts, or with a dinosaur model. Use wire to string the bones together, and try to bend them various ways—you'll "feel" what movements the dinosaur could have made.

You have to learn to weld and work steel if you want to put a dinosaur together yourself. (Ed Gerken)

Dinosaurs can't go on vacation unless they can come apart and be packed in sections. (Ed Gerken)

based plastic called "water putty." It works like plaster of paris, but is much more durable. You can use plaster of paris, too, but it's not very strong.

All putties can be colored with pigments, or painted, to match the original bones. It's important *not* to make it *exactly* the same color, because scientists have to know which parts are fake. This may be the only time when you want your art to be *nearly* perfect. You want to be a great preparator, but not a counterfeiter.

After cleaning and restoring bones, you'll want to apply a thin, final coat of PVA. It will block out water, air and junk in the air, oil and acids found on your probing fingers, or the sticky, fizzy, nasty soda your little brother just spilled.

"Is It Real?"

Cast replicas are essential to paleontology because not everyone can go to the Smithsonian or the American Museum of Natural History, or to our

< 90 >

Legos are the perfect material for building molding boxes—they're even reusable. Here our crew is making the mold *(left)*, then removing the cast part—which looks just like the original bone. (Terry Wentz)

museum in South Dakota, to see the coolest fossils. If we make casts, then copies of dinosaurs that are *almost exactly like the originals* can go on tour or on permanent display in museums around the world. It's almost like making a clone of the original fossil.

People have been casting almost as long as there have been people. They've made jewelry and spear heads, and toys and dinosaur skeletons. They've used beeswax and clay, metals, plasters, and plastic. When we're making fossil replicas, we have to be especially careful in the products and techniques we use, because what we're copying is very delicate.

When we want to make a copy of a fossil, there are two parts to the process:

1. Making the mold.
2. Pouring the cast.

The idea is to make a shell around the fossil, one side at a time, and then fill the shell with rubber or silicone to make the copy that picks up the tiniest details. Using *polyurethane resin* will create a strong cast that reproduces everything—each small crack, each chip, each injury.

One cool thing about casts: when you want to put a whole dinosaur together, a fake one can be drilled or cut so steel supports can go inside. We

< 91 >

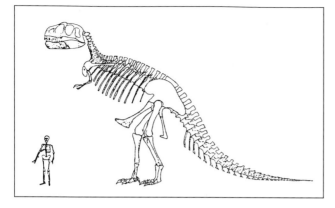

The first drawing of a *T. rex* skeleton, made in 1905. (H.F. Osborn)

In the middle of the 1800s, this is what people imagined dinosaurs to be. (From Richardson et al., circa 1860, *The Museum of Natural History*, plate 7.)

try to avoid drilling real fossil bones—unless they are extremely common. Some duckbill dinosaurs, for example, were so plentiful they are sometimes called Cretaceous "sheep." However, with one-of-a-kind or significant skeletons, like a *T. rex*, we want each and every bone to remain unharmed and removable for study. With real bones, the steel supports go on the outside.

When we're putting together a fossil, called *mounting*, our job is to make the creature look "alive" and as if it is moving. As if someone just happened to catch it in the middle of its dinner, or having a walk—and then stripped off all its skin and meat.

The very first dinosaur skeletons were mounted in the second half of the 1800s. The first *T. rex* finally stood up in 1915, at the American Museum of Natural History in New York. For decades and decades, these fossils were paleontology's examples. And as we all know by now, science changes as new facts and details are discovered. Those skeletons had lots of mistakes, and lots of paleontologists repeated them over and over. I know I did.

To be fair, it wasn't really anybody's fault. In the beginning, few dinosaur skeletons had been found, so how in the world was anyone supposed to know all the details? Sometimes they didn't *have* all the bones, and sometimes they didn't *see* exactly what they had. Plus, those first scientists suffered from a very common illness: monster-itis. They just wanted their creatures to look BIG and SCARY.

After building skeletons at our museums for a while, Ken and I noticed some common mistakes in old dinosaur mounts. Anyway, we believe they were mistakes. One was how the hands are positioned. Lots of specimens have their palms facing down, like a dog's when it's begging for a treat. Another was the chest: the shoulder blades were pushed back and apart, so the chest was wide and the arms out to the sides.

Just like those first scientists, I didn't know better. The first dinosaurs I mounted looked that way, too. We learned of our mistakes through a couple of observations. As more dinosaurs were found, more of them had their parts articulated. We started to find fossils with their shoulders, arms, and hands in place—and we saw the way they really went together. Also, we looked at

< 92 >

Ken and I don't think this is the correct way to mount *T. rex* shoulder blades. You can see here that they are more than a foot apart. (Peter Larson)

living animals with similar body structures—usually birds—and noticed how their skeletons worked. Generally, dinosaur hands would have their palms facing each other—as if the creature were holding a basketball. And the chest would be narrow, with the shoulder blades nearly touching in the front. Of course, this seemed to be a case of the *Triceratops* Two-Step Revisited. Not all scientists agree with this, and the debate will undoubtedly rage on for years.

Another mistake is easier to see. You know when you see a *T. rex* or a duckbill in a museum standing up on its two hind legs like a kangaroo, using its tail as a kickstand? We don't do that anymore, but only because of all the new information we've uncovered since 1915. The truth is, to make a duckbill stand like a kangaroo, you

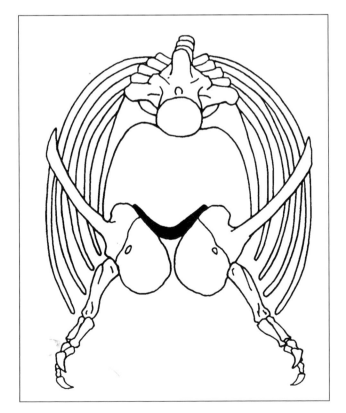

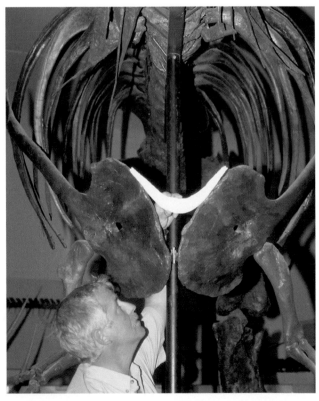

The newest scientific thinking puts *T. rex* shoulder blades nearly touching, below the wishbone. (Left: Dorothy Sigler Norton; Right: Peter Larson)

< 93 >

Sea Monsters

Way before dinosaurs were described and talked about, visitors to the coast of Lyme Regis in the south of England would see a young girl hunting for fossils around the base of the cliffs. Mary Anning was collecting ammonites and sea creatures. She was also about to change the world.

Mary's parents had a fossil business, and in 1810 her father died. By then, Mary was only eleven years old, but she helped support her mother and older brother by selling her fossils to tourists. She was a professional collector, but she was more than that. When she was twelve, Mary's older brother Joseph found the world's first ichthyosaur, a dolphinlike reptile. Mary actually collected it, and because she recognized it as something unique, history books give her credit for the discovery. She later found and excavated the world's first plesiosaur, which looks kind of like a giant turtle with a snake stuck through it. If there ever was a Loch Ness Monster, this was it.

Fossil collecting not only gave Mary money to live on, but it also fired her hunger for knowledge. She visited the British Museum and libraries where she copied—by hand—scientific papers and drawings. She even trained herself to analyze her finds—she identified fossil cuttlefish, a type of squid, by dissecting modern ones. Eventually, she took over the family business, and many scientists came to buy fossils and to ask her questions about geology and anatomy.

A pleisiosaur's pointy teeth were good for catching fish. (Layne Kennedy)

Mary was one of the first paleontologists ever. She figured out how to do paleontology all by herself. In England, there's a fossil club called the Mary Anning Society, and the tongue-twister "She sells seashells by the seashore" was written about her. When you think about it, that tongue-twister seems pretty tame. Some of the creatures she collected reached more than sixty feet long, and some had large and snaggly teeth.

Seashells. As *if*. But I guess it sounded better than "She sells sea *monsters* by the seashore."

This pleisiosaur from Lyme Regis is like the one Mary Anning first discovered. (Neal Larson)

A rare tail drag on a duckbill dinosaur trackway. If you look closely, you'll notice front and rear footprints walking toward you—the tail drag is the line along the left. (Peter Larson)

have to force the hip socket apart. To curl a *T. rex* tail enough for it to work like a kickstand, we have to move the bones in ways they just don't want to go.

One other piece of evidence—of the Type II variety—supports what the Type I bones tell us. In trackways that show dozens or even hundreds of footprints, there is almost no evidence of "tail dragging." We almost never find a line in the mud that could have been caused by a big, heavy tail that dragged behind a creature as it walked.

On rare occasions we do find a tail drag, so we think it's a special occasion. Maybe a creature who made such a mark had a broken tail. Or maybe we're not really seeing a "tail drag" at all—maybe it's a "mammal drag" or a "crocodile drag." Maybe this creative dinosaur had to eat on the run and was dragging its dinner along by its ear. Bounce, drag, bounce.

Since the original *T. rex* was mounted in the goofy Godzilla way, generations of people saw him as a slow, stupid dinosaur. A reptile that hung out all day in a swamp, lazily watching giant dragonflies buzz by. Picking his teeth with a rib from his last meal.

Well, now we know better.

I don't care how TALL and SCARY people thought the "old" *T. rex* was. To me, the "new" *T. rex* is way more exciting. It's way scarier when it's crouched low, running after someone, head inches from its victim, teeth bared for a

< 95 >

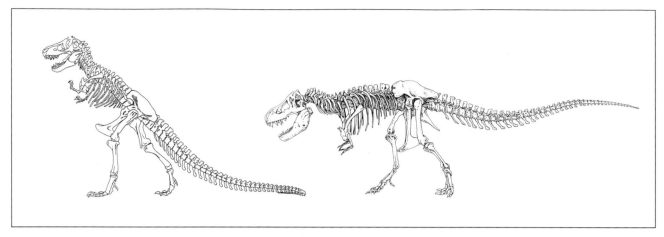

The old and new postures for _T. rex._ (Left: H.F. Osborn; Right: Dorothy Sigler Norton)

bite. We don't have to bend it out of shape to make it look awesome.

And speaking of awesome, does a cast of a fossil ever look as cool as a real one? Whether we're talking about just one bone, or a whole skeleton, most people automatically say, "No! I want to see the real thing." Truthfully, though, they usually can't tell the difference. But you can!

Secret Tip: There are two main fake-detecting techniques that you can use with no special equipment, no ultraviolet lights, and no touching of the fossil. You just need your eyes.

Remember the casting process? The part where we cut and drill the fake bones and put metal _inside_ them? But where real bones usually have their metal supports on the _outside_? Well, the first clue is: can you see lots of metal, or just a little metal? Next, real bones are _much_ heavier than fake ones. So the second clue is: how many poles are holding up the dinosaur? If there are tall ones under the head, the hips, and the tail, it's probably heavy—and real. If there are just little sticks poking out of the bottom of the feet, it's a clone.

Mystery: _T. rex_ Time

Okay. I promised to tell you about this. I thought you'd forget, but since your brain is young and juicy, you didn't. It takes about 25,000 hours of skilled preparation to clean a whole _T. rex._ If you were an expert preparator, and you were working all by yourself, it would take you twelve and a half years. It's a gigantic job. By the time you finished, _you'd_ be a fossil. If we have our whole staff working hard, we can do it in one or two years. I recommend having a staff.

< 96 >

Above: This real *Maiasaura* skeleton was mounted as if it were lying dead on its side. Notice all of the steel supports. (Neal Larson) *Right:* A close-up of how the steel is shaped to cradle individual foot bones. (Peter Larson)

A cast skeleton may be mounted with almost no visible steel. (Ed Gerken)

< 97 >

Can you tell the difference in these *Albertosaurus* cast feet? One is good and one is not so good. (Ed Gerken)

The second technique is to look carefully at the bones. Real bones come in all different colors, depending on the minerals that washed into them underground. They all started out as white, and some may still be. Others will come in almost any color you can think of: yellow, red, brown, black, and sometimes blue or green! No matter what the color, the casts should be a slightly different shade. The very best casts can look really close to the original color, but many others aren't as high quality. Sometimes if you just compare different bones, you can instantly tell by either color or texture which one is plastic.

With a little practice, you'll be able to tell if something's real, and if a cast is good! Pretty soon, you'll get very snooty about it. You'll say to your friends, "Ugh, that's a *terrible* cast, and it's *poorly mounted*." They may roll their eyes, but you *know* they'll ask how you can tell. And you'll sound like a real paleontologist when you answer.

CODE WORDS

Ammonites

Cast replica

Clay

Claystone

Clone, cloned

Fluoresce, fluorescent

Infrared light

Matrix

Mounting

Preparation, preparator

Reconstruction

Sand

Sandstone

Silt

Siltstone

Soil

Tail drag

Ultraviolet light

< 98 >

Stan's Plans

By now you're an expert at *finding* a fossil, *preparing* it in the laboratory, *casting* it, and even designing how you'll *mount* it. Here's a whole new challenge. In Chapter 1, I asked you several questions, like whether a *Brachiosaurus* chewed its food, or whether a *T. rex* could see you even if you stood still, or swallow a whole lawyer in one gulp. The absolute truth is: we don't know.

But we *love* to guess! And we have the tools to do it. We've dug them up and we've cleaned them. The more tools we find, the better our guesses become.

The solid evidence of paleontology is the fossil record. People take the evidence and study it: we trace muscle scars, we measure femurs, we calculate brain size. But the next step—family life, or behavior, or mating calls, or whether *Stegosaurus* played cards—these might never be proved completely.

We may never be able to climb up a tree and peek through our binoculars at a herd of *Edmontosaurus* or a family of *T. rex*. But we can make educated guesses—those hypotheses and theories—about how they lived. We may never watch an *Oviraptor* lay eggs, but we do find fossilized parents sitting on their nests. Even though we might some day know *exactly* how a *Triceratops* moved its front legs, we might never know what color its skin was.

The *facts* we find in the earth lead to questions. Answering them sometimes sends us out on a limb. Or under our beds.

The Bare Bones

"My, What a Big *Head* You Have!"

I can't decide. Was it cooler to find Sue's complete skull in the field, or cooler to put together the never-before-seen insides of a *T. rex*

< 99 >

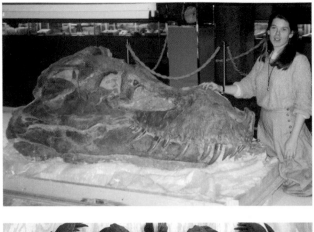

Sue's skull came out of the ground in one piece (that's co-author Kristin with her) (Terry Wentz); Stan's skull was completely disarticulated. (Ed Gerken)

India's Bedroom

I've seen the Denver Museum of Nature and Science's *Allosaurus* plenty of times. I've looked at it and admired it. But for the longest time I didn't know it had begun its life as a "discovered" fossil under a bed. Well, not *just* under the bed. "Bones were under the bed, on the desk, on the windowsill, covering the bookshelf," recalls India Wood. "They were everywhere."

India was thirteen. She was on her spring break, as usual visiting family friends who ran a ranch in Colorado not far from Dinosaur National Monument. By then, she was an expert fossil hunter, because the ranch woman didn't like kids under her feet. "She always sent us outside, snipe hunting, or looking for arrowheads or bones." For years, India had been digging fossils, including some good-sized bones, with a rock hammer and a screwdriver. And even before that, she'd dug up ammonites on the golf course near her house in Colorado Springs.

Meanwhile, back at the ranch, on one particular 1979 summer day, she saw a little piece of bone sticking out from the sediment. It kept going back into the hill, and she kept

skull in the laboratory? Each one is great in its own way.

Every paleontologist I know loves it when the curve of a skull bone of any fabulous dinosaur first peeks out of the ground. They love how it looks when they dig further and further, following the trail of bone—until what seemed to be just one bone has become a just-about-perfect whole skull. Sure, it's cracked and maybe warped a little, but you know what I mean. All together, articulated, right there in the ground. When I got my first good look at Sue's skull, I thought I'd died and gone to heaven.

But Stan's skull was something else, and it was not quite as perfect. Or so I thought.

Stan is the second *T. rex* we dug and, if my theory is correct, he's the largest male ever found. He has almost as many bones as Sue, and we find a few more each time we widen the dig site. Soon he may catch up to her and become the most complete.

At first I was disappointed by Stan's skull, because it was in a million pieces. Well, to be

< 100 >

digging it out. The preservation was very good, but the bone was broken in many places. In the field, India glued the little pieces together, and then wrapped the bigger chunks in cloth to take home.

India in her collecting heyday. (Nancy Wood)

India had no mentor, and she didn't know anyone from a rock club. She didn't know anybody who wanted to discuss her favorite subject with her. Or tell her about the best glues to use. All by herself, she stuck her bone together—with Elmer's, not a bad choice!—until it was back in its original shape. Then she went to the library and looked at drawings of bones until she thought she'd spotted hers. It turns out that her first bone came

from the pelvis, and was called the ilium. What India didn't know is that the ilium is especially different in different animals. It just so happens that India had a bone that looked unusual enough that she could match it with one of the drawings.

She thought she had an *Allosaurus*.

By the time she was sixteen, India had been back and forth on break for three more summers, and her room was filling up with eighteen bones from the same dinosaur! Finally, her mom told her to clean up the mess. So on a Friday, India drove a box of bones over to the Denver Museum. On Monday a paleontologist called her on the phone. He couldn't believe his eyes.

You probably won't believe this, but next she said, "If you want my bones, I'd like you to give me a job." And for the next two sum-mers, India escorted the paleontologists to her dig site and they helped her dig out her dinosaur; the summer after that, she worked at the museum's paleo lab.

Just for the record, she was right. It *was* an *Allosaurus*. Next time you're in Denver, stop by and have a look at it. It's magnificent.

exact, thirty-nine pieces, not counting loose teeth and some breaks we made taking the blocks apart. I had been spoiled by Sue's skull, and I thought her all-in-one-piece way was the best way to find a skull, but it's not true. Don't tell Sue this, but Stan has the best *T. rex* skull ever—and part of the reason is because it was scattered apart in the ground. I didn't under-

stand how cool it was until we put it back together in the lab.

Okay, I decided. It's the same amount of cool-ness to find a Sue skull or a Stan skull. In both cases, my hands and my eyes discovered some-thing new, and they told my brain about it. That's when the Big Ideas flooded in.

The Big Ideas that happen in the lab—like

< 101 >

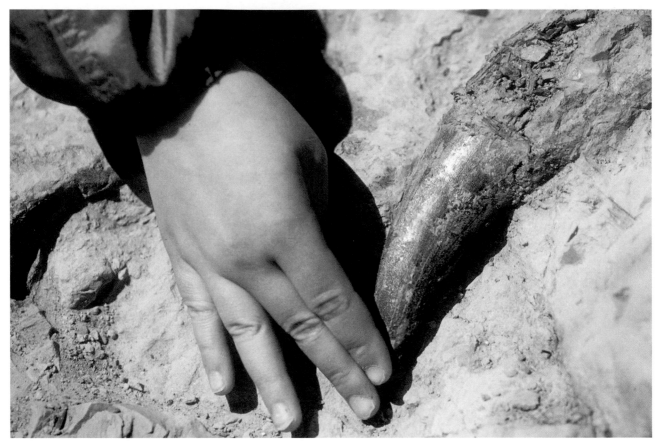

Touching a 65-million-year-old Stan's tooth, while it's still in the ground. (Layne Kennedy)

they did with Stan's skull—are special, because you can lay everything out and take a good look at it. Once the bones are cleaned, you can see exactly what's there and what's missing. Sometimes it takes a while to see what the evidence means, but with practice, you get better at finding tiny clues. This is when you can *really* start to see into the past, into the life of the animal.

To see the tiny clues, we start with the big, obvious clues. See if you agree with the ones I found on Stan. You might find others!

"My, What Big *Teeth* You Have!"

Teeth are easy to think about. They're easy to see, and they're hard, so they hang around longer than most fossil parts. In the field, even a tooth that's not fully cleaned can give you lots of information. The jagged edges of a *T. rex* or *Nanotyrannus* tooth are easy to feel with your finger. You can tell if the tooth was broken off or not by seeing whether its root is in place. (Remember? Whole or half banana.) And we can tell whose tooth it was, assuming we can compare it to one still in a skull. But what else can we learn about the creatures who used to be attached to these teeth?

Probably the first thing is what they ate. Just think about it: if you had a mouthful of thick knives, like a *Nanotyrannus*, how would they work? Would they be the same teeth a cow uses today to chew its cud? Would they work like a

< 102 >

Camarasaurus, Triceratops, and *T. rex* all had different shaped teeth for different purposes. (Peter Larson)

Saber-toothed cats can only cut with their teeth. However, giant pigs—some of their molars are pictured in the foreground—have different kinds of teeth in their mouth. Sharper front ones are used for poking around looking for food, and then grabbing it; molars in the back grind up the food. (Peter Larson)

Triceratops's teeth? Or more like a saber-toothed cat's?

Once we know a tooth's *job,* bingo! We know something about the behavior of the creature wearing it.

Okay. You know about teeth, because you have some. The ones in front are used for cutting food and, of course, pulling out staples. (I don't encourage this. We have tools and opposable thumbs for this purpose—and we get only one set of permanent teeth!) Cutting teeth are your sharpest teeth. If you had to chew all your food with your front teeth, just imagine how hard that would be. They would keep *cutting* the food, but they wouldn't *grind* it up. The ones used for grinding and mashing are in the back. They are flat instead of sharp. They are wide, to provide a good mashing surface. The more teeth are used, the more worn down they get. We can look at a dinosaur's teeth—or anybody else's, for that matter—to tell how much cutting or mashing they do.

Many animals have more than one kind of tooth in their heads, because there's more than one job to be done. Cutting, then mashing, for example. Biting off grass or corn from the cob, then mashing it. A horse. A raccoon. A person.

T. rex has only one style of tooth. All his teeth have the same basic shape, although they come in different sizes and thicknesses. There are no flat-topped, mashing ones. What does this mean? *No chewing! No mashing!*

Wow! No chewing? Can you imagine *that?* We chew automatically, without even thinking about it. What would happen if you couldn't chew? If all your teeth were made only to cut? No bubble gum, that's for sure. The idea of swallowing *chunks* of something without chewing seems gross. But why? It seems gross to me because of my digestive system. Because of my throat and how the doctor's Popsicle stick—the one she uses to hold down my tongue to look at my sore tonsils—sometimes makes me gag. If a *T. rex* had a mouth and throat and stomach and

< 103 >

If Sue were still alive today, my kids wouldn't stand this close to those pointy, cutting teeth. (This picture was taken in 1992, when my kids were your age!) (Ed Gerken)

intestines like ours, *he would have had different teeth.*

See how cool this is? We can't see a *T. rex*'s insides, but we can get a good idea of what his guts were like just by thinking about what we *can* see—or feel.

Also, we can look at other animals' bodies, live ones that carry around a mouthful of teeth similar to a *T. rex*'s. Are dogs a good example? Well, kind

Lions make a pretty good *T. rex* model. (Peter Larson)

of, because they have cutting teeth, but they also have mashing teeth. Bears? Nope, mostly mashing. Lions? Much better. Almost all their teeth are for cutting, but still not a perfect model. Dogs, bears, and lions can all chew.

Two creatures I can think of with no chewing teeth at all are crocodiles and sharks. How do they eat? Crocodiles have strong jaws filled with short puncturing teeth. They

< 104 >

Crocodile teeth don't really cut, but they're strong enough to poke holes in bones. (Richard Fagan)

bite and hold on, and they shake their victim into pieces—and then they swallow it, chunk by chunk. Definitely no chewing, but not really cutting either. Also not very attractive. Sharks actually do more cutting. We've found (sorry, but it's true) whole victims inside crocodiles' and sharks' bellies, maybe in a couple of pieces. Imagine the damage a *T. rex* could do, when the cutting part of each big tooth is six inches long? We've found big, strong leg bones of other dinosaurs *cut in half*, with marks that match a *T. rex* tooth. I'm absolutely positive Sue could eat a lawyer. She might bite him in half, but really, how hard would that be? Not very, with giant jaws that work like shears—and lawyers are pretty soft in the middle. Everyone is.

This *T. rex* lower leg bone (tibia) was bitten in half. Notice the rough break at the top—this happened while the bone was still fresh. (Ed Gerken)

< 105 >

Okay, enough of this disgusting carnage. Let's move directly to the more peaceful types—like a deer. Is anyone less scary than Bambi, gently chewing a breakfast snack of clover? What about a camel? I've heard they spit a lot while they chew. We've all seen a cow or a horse while it's chewing. Even a chipmunk or a squirrel in the park. Their little mouths go chomp, chomp, chomp, sometimes with their lower jaws moving kind of in a circular motion. Mashing.

So does it make sense that the *Brachiosaurus* in *Jurassic Park* would strip leaves off a tree and chew them right in front of that girl? (We'll discuss the sneezing part in a minute.)

To figure out whether the *Brachiosaurus* would chew, we look at its teeth. They are kind of blunt—halfway between cutting and mashing. Since they don't show the kind of wear we'd expect from a masher, probably *Brachiosaurus* ate in a third kind of way. They used their teeth to grasp leaves and pull them from trees, swallowing them whole. The mashing happened in the stomach, where the leaves were ground up by gizzard stones. These are little rocks they would have swallowed just for that purpose—that's how some birds do it, too. We know *Brachiosaurus* did it because of their teeth, and because we find these polished gizzard stones with long-necked skeletons. In birds, gizzard stones are called, well, gizzard stones. In dinosaurs, gizzard stones are also called *gastroliths*, and sometimes they make good gemstones.

Okay, so now by looking at teeth we can tell:

1. Whether a creature only bit its food, perhaps pulling it apart, or if it could cut and mash.

2. Something about the digestive system of a creature. Was it simple or complex? Should we look for gizzard stones?

These gizzard stones were found in the Morrison Formation and once ground up food in the belly of a long-neck. (Peter Larson)

< 106 >

About the sneezing, it turns out that *Brachiosaurus* had quite a large nasal passage. If one had, say, hay fever, she could probably blow out about one half gallon of snot with a good sneeze.

Eeeeeww.

"My, What a Fine *Brain* You Have!"

A *T. rex* skull is made of more than fifty separate bones, and we found most of Stan's skull bones individually. Because of a miracle of preservation, each piece was in great shape. It had never occurred to me what might happen in a case like this. Since we were finding pieces from *inside* a *T. rex* skull, they were pieces no one had ever seen before.

Until Stan's skull, the only way we could look inside a complete skull was to break it open—which might permanently damage such a special fossil—or to use technology, such as CAT scans.

CAT scans are awesome, but there's nothing like a 3-D puzzle right under your fingertips. With Stan, we were able to see exactly how the *inside* of the skull fit together, in person. We got to see details and joints no one had ever laid eyes on before, delicate folds of bone that intertwined with adjoining bones. They were beautiful, and so fragile I felt like I could break them just by looking at them too hard.

We also got to trace the pathways used by Stan's nerves, the equipment that connected his nose and eyes and mouth to his brain. Although

The latest dinosaur skull we peeked inside is a *Gorgosaurus*. In my left hand, I'm holding the ethmoid, a bone that separates sections of the smelling part of the brain. In my right hand is the lid of the brain case—the rest of the brain case is on the left. (Ed Gerken)

< 107 >

Cool Tool: CAT Scan

X-rays allow us to look inside a fossil without touching it. We can see internal structures or pathologies of individual bones. Sometimes whole fossil fish, birds, or bats are trapped inside lake sediments. We can look inside the rock, which is usually preserved in thin sheets. We even can take pictures with X-rays, if we put film under the fossil and then X-ray it from the top.

X-ray images are "flat," though, and sometimes we want to see in three dimensions, or 3-D. With Computer Axial Tomography, or CAT scans, we can rotate around the object, making X-ray "slices" at regular stops. These slices are put back together in a computer to produce a 3-D image that can be rotated on the screen.

CAT scans allow us to "cut open" the bones to see what is inside without doing any damage. They also allow us to look at brain cavities, nerve pathways, inner ear structures, and more features we otherwise could not see without breaking the bone apart.

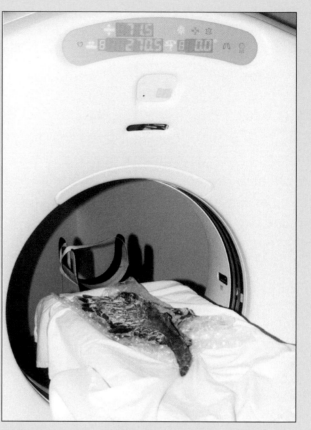

CAT scanning a maxilla bone from a *Gorgosaurus* nose. Our mission was to locate tiny sinus bones before preparation, and we looked at hundreds of images. CAT scan use was provided courtesy of Rapid City Regional Hospital. (Peter Larson)

---

the nerves, spinal cord, and brain tissue are long gone, the holes that held those "cables" and that "computer" are still there, and we can make some conclusions about how Stan used his brain and nerves and senses. Since we've also found good skulls of other types of dinosaurs, we can then compare Stan's abilities to everybody else's.

In general, the bigger the brain, the smarter the creature. This comparison works in *overall* size—a tick is less smart than an elephant, because the elephant's brain is so much bigger.

The comparison also works in *relative* size. Relative means the comparison between the size of the brain and the size of the body it's in. Two creatures might have about the same size of brain, but really different sizes of bodies. An Australian saltwater crocodile—the largest living crocodile, which maxes out at about eighteen feet long—has a brain about the same size as a house cat's. But they're not the same when it comes to smarts. Cats can figure out lots of things that crocs can't, like that if they sit on

< 108 >

This is Stan's brain case. My finger is pointing to the exit for the optic nerve—as it made its way to his eye. (Peter Larson)

your homework when you're trying to do it you'll be *really* annoyed. If you compared the size of the croc's brain to his whole body *and* the size of the cat's brain to his whole body, you would see that the croc brain is *relatively* much smaller. It takes up a smaller part of its body than the cat's brain uses in the cat—and the cat is smarter. It's all in the math.

Both overall size and relative size are important when we compare the smarts or abilities of various creatures. But there's more to our math equation. The word "relative" can work in another way. The brain isn't just one big chunk. It has different parts that do different things—so in one single animal, one part, like thinking, might be *relatively* bigger than other parts.

< 109 >

A cat's thinking part is bigger than the croc's thinking part. All brains are not created equal.

Let's start with something we all know first-hand. Dogs are good smellers, and they use this sense to hunt for food. This means:

1. The smelling part of a dog's brain is relatively big compared to other parts of its *own* brain.
2. The smelling part of a dog's brain is relatively big compared to the smelling parts in other creatures who don't need to smell as well as dogs, like fish.

Vultures are good watchers. They eat dead things, and they have to look for them from high in the sky, so they have to see well. Their eyes are on the sides of their heads, which means they can see fine in front of them but especially well out to the side—about twice as much of what's happening around them as we can.

Now that you know the dog example, I bet you can draw some conclusions about a vulture's brain:

1. The seeing part of a vulture's brain is relatively big compared to the other parts of its own brain.
2. The seeing part of a vulture's brain is relatively big compared to the seeing parts in creatures who don't need to see as well as vultures, like moles.

Dogs and vultures are alive. We can study their brains and compare their relative skills. But how does this stuff help us understand dinosaurs? They're extinct, and bacteria ate their brains millions of years ago. What could we possibly know about dinosaur brains?

Tons.

How do you tell how smart somebody is? Or how well he could see? If the creature is *alive* right now, you can just look at the brain, through X-rays. If the creature was very recently alive, you can look at its brain directly. You can cut it up and weigh it and stuff like that. Yuck. The brain has different parts that do different things—smelling, thinking—and we can see which parts are bigger. The thinking part is called the *cerebrum* in mammals and birds and theropod dinosaurs. If that was big, the creature was smart.

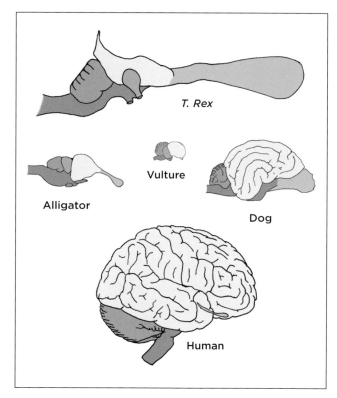

You can see how different brains are organized, and how they are better at different stuff.

Optic Lobe (sight) = blue.
Olfactory Bulb (smell) = green.
Cerebrum (thinking) = yellow.
Cerebellum (balance and coordination) = orange.
Brain Stem (heart beat, breathing, reflexes) = red.

The Optic Lobes for dogs and humans are quite small— and embedded so you can't see them. [Peter Larson, after Brooke, M. & Birkhead, T., 1991 (vulture), Evans, H.E. & de Lahunta, A., 1988 (dog), Kardong, K.V., 1998 (alligator), Marieb, E.N. & Mallatt, J., 1992 (human), and Osborn, 1912 (T. rex).]

< 110 >

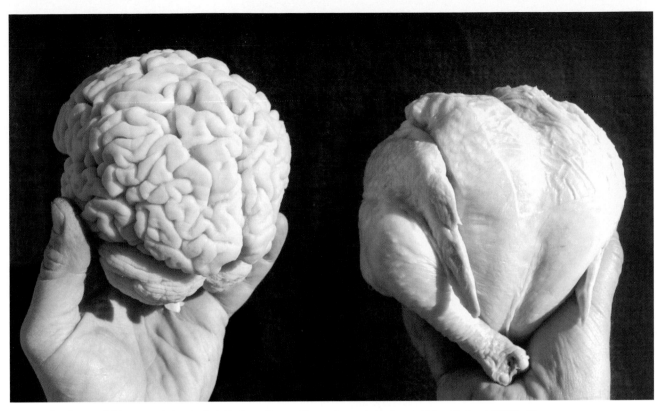

A *T.rex* brain would have weighed slightly less than either a human brain or this chicken! (Peter Larson)

But what about creatures whose brains are all gone? We can look only at the structure that held their brains, the *brain case*. And the holes that carried the nerves back and forth. We know which parts of all brains generally go where—and which parts of the brain took up more relative space than other parts. Did the nose get more brain power? Or the eyes? How big was the cerebrum?

In order to "weigh" a dinosaur brain, the closest we can come is to measure the volume of the brain case. If we pour liquid into a cast of Stan's brain case, we see that it takes about 1000 cubic centimeters (cc) to fill it up. That's about a quart of milk. It would have weighed a little over two pounds.

Stan's brain was bigger than the brains of his dinner—duckbills and *Triceratops*. In fact, he

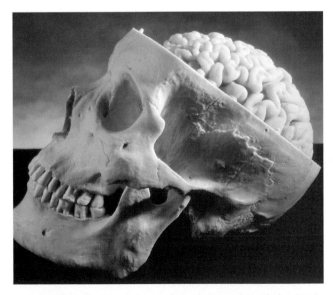

Nobody's brain takes up each and every bit of the brain case. (Layne Kennedy)

and his kind had the biggest brain cases of all the dinosaurs. Does that mean Stan was the smartest dinosaur? Alas, it isn't that simple.

< 111 >

Got Milk? Measuring the volume of a brain case is a pretty accurate way to gauge the size of the brain that was in it. (Layne Kennedy)

< 112 >

Your brain and my brain measure between 1,200 and 1,800 cc, and weigh between 2.5 and 4 pounds. Our brains are bigger than Stan's. But an elephant's is bigger than ours—5,000 cc, or 12 pounds! As much as a solid watermelon. And more than you weighed when you were born.

It might be easy for us to think at first that overall size wins, but if that were true, an elephant would be much smarter—*much smarter*—than you. Just like with dog noses and vulture eyes, overall brain size is not enough to tell what a dinosaur was good at. Let's look at the relative information before we decide how smart Stan was.

The largest part—more than half!—of *T. rex*'s brain was for smell. What does good smelling do for a creature? We know that dogs use smell to hunt for food and vultures don't. Why not? Vultures, which are scavengers, almost never have a good sense of smell—because what they are looking for is already dead, and gross and smelly. If Stan's sniffer was good, this means his nose would work more like a dog's than a vulture's. His sniffer was so good, in fact, it would work more like a dog's *than a dog's*.

Another large brain part was for sight. The eye sockets were big compared to the size of the skull *and* compared to the eye sockets of other creatures—even those living today. In fact, *T. rex* had room for the largest eye of any land animal. Also, the holes in the skull that carried the nerves from the eyes to the brain as big as my thumb. This means its eyes would work well.

Now, my idea is that if Stan had such a large eye, and such big "cables" going to it, probably this eye was very high-tech. I'm betting that Stan could see in color, like his living rela-

Both this baby and this watermelon weigh about the same amount as an elephant's brain! (Peter Larson)

tives—birds and crocodiles—and with the clarity of an eagle. Plus, because both eyes faced forward, he could judge distance, or *depth of field*. The only way any creature can do that is if both its eyes face forward—*binocular vision*, the mark of a hunter. Eagles have binocular vision, and so do dogs, cats, and people. But not *Triceratops*, iguanas, bison, or vultures.

< 113 >

Because their eyes are placed differently on their heads, prey animals (top) would see this herd of buffalo differently from predatory animals (bottom). (Layne Kennedy)

I think it's safe to say that *T. rex* could hunt, chase his dinner, and make decisions about distances, dangers, and depths—watch out for that cliff! *I'm betting he could see that kid in the movie, whether the kid was standing still or not.* But perhaps even more important, he could smell him. Stan could have guessed that boy's weight and height, along with knowing what he'd had for lunch and what he accidentally stepped on when he got out of the car. That kid was a pudding cup just waiting to happen.

Okay, so Stan could do his hunting job really well. But does that mean he was *smart*? Relative to the size of his whole brain, Stan's cerebrum—the thinking part—is pretty small. Bummer.

Of all dinosaurs, *Velociraptor* and other rap-

< 114 >

tors, including the smallest one, *Bambiraptor*, had the largest cerebrums relative to their brain size. So even though their *overall* brain size was smaller than *T. rex*'s, they probably were smarter. Stan was busy using his brain to smell you. *Velociraptor* was ready to play chess with you (before dinner!).

So Stan was no Einstein. But was he as dumb as a box of rocks?

Stan weighed about four tons. Some of the long-necks, like *Diplodocus*, weighed about twelve tons. *Diplodocus*'s brain capacity was about 100 cc—just a couple of gulps of milk.

Let's do more math:

12 *Diplodocus* tons ÷ 4 Stan tons = 3.

A *Diplodocus* weighed 3 times more than a *T. rex*.

1000 Stan cubic centimeters ÷ 100 *Diplodocus* cubic centimeters = 10.

A *T. rex*'s brain was 10 times larger than a *Diplodocus*'s.

That poor *Diplodocus*. He was way huger and his brain was way tinier. He *was* as dumb as a box of rocks! *T. rex* was Einstein compared to the long-necks—or should we call them pea-brains?

But what about animals alive today? How would Stan compare if he were alive right now? The thinking part in a human brain is bigger than *T. rex*'s. That should make you happy: you're smarter than a *T. rex*, even if he could swallow you whole.

An elephant weighs four tons, just like a *T. rex*. His watermelon-sized brain is five times larger than *T. rex*'s. His thinking part is relatively big, too. Sure, a *T. rex* could smell and see and maneuver better than an elephant, but an elephant does everything else better. An ele-

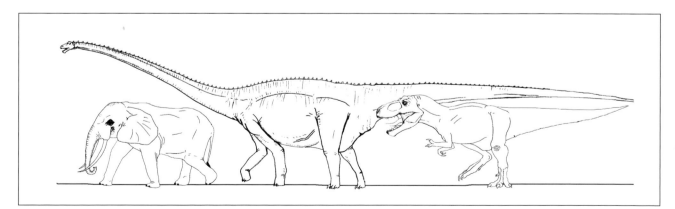

The biggest is not necessarily the smartest! (Chris Ott, Neal Andrew Larson, Matt Larson)

< 115 >

"Now, where did I put my lawyer?"

Comparing brain parts. Comparing smelling and seeing and thinking. These are generally solid methods of creating guesses, the theories about how an extinct creature functioned. By knowing how living animals function, we can get good, solid ideas.

These ideas could happen in the laboratory or in the library. A good idea might even come to you while you are not paying attention in Social Studies—or while you *are* paying attention. Scientists have written about the cubic centimeters of living animals' brains, they've measured their teeth, and they've recorded their behavior. We can research almost anything, either by reading or by asking the experts in the field. If we have an elephant question, we ask the elephant guy. Or we can search the Internet.

The next part of thinking about science takes us one more step into our imaginations. We're going to take what we already know about brains, along with living animal models, and *guess* how an extinct animal acted when it was alive. Let's look at a subject that paleontologists are arguing about right now. We love those.

phant can use tools—he can pick up tree limbs to scratch himself, or to yank down other tree limbs for eating. He can play well with others— *T. rex* would probably cause trouble in a circus ring—and because the cerebrum also is where emotions are produced, an elephant can *feel*. Not only would he be smarter than Stan—than the raptors, too—but also he could be happy or sad about it. An elephant never forgets, but a *T. rex* probably did.

Behavior

So now we can see how preparing the delicate, wondrous bones of Stan's skull led us on a whole trek through time, comparing brain size.

The Menu

Did *T. rex* eat roadkill, or did he hunt? Was he a giant garbage disposal, or the King of the Cretaceous?

First, let's list the stuff a roadkill eater, or a *scavenger*, needs to find dead things:

1. Good eyes.
2. Some ability to smell dead, rotting, nasty carcasses.
3. A way to cover lots of territory.
4. Tools to eat its food.

< 116 >

Scavenger. (Noel Snyder, Courtesy of the U.S. Fish and Wildlife Service)

Predator. (Bill Brent)

Now, let's list the stuff a hunter, or a *predator*, needs to kill things:

1. Good eyes to see its prey, especially to judge distance.
2. Good nose for tracking.
3. Speed or smarts enough to catch its food.
4. Tools to kill its food.

Let's look at a turkey vulture as the Scavenger example, and a lion as the Predator example. Unlike other vultures, the turkey vulture has a relatively large smelling part in its brain. This means both our Scavenger and Predator have pretty good sniffers—and both have good eyes. The vulture can cover hundreds of square miles in one day, by flying in the air. Although it can see widely, it can't judge distance. The lion has to walk everywhere, but its hunter eyes are good with distance. Both creatures have tools to deal with their dinners. Claws, beaks, or teeth. But the lion has excellent tools for killing her victims: she runs fast and uses her claws and teeth to drag her dinner down.

We know *T. rex* had good eyes and nose, gnarly teeth and claws. So our question is: did he find dead stuff, or chase down live stuff? Was he

fast enough to catch duckbills and *Triceratops*?

A famous scientist in Montana, Jack Horner, thinks *T. rex* didn't run fast enough to catch *Triceratops* or duckbills. He figured the *T. rex*'s lower leg bones were too short to make a fast runner's legs. If that's true, Stan would have had

Tools of the trade: mountain lion teeth and *T. rex* claws. (Peter Larson)

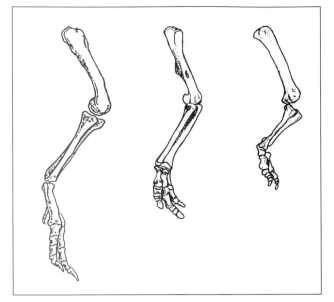

From left to right, *T. rex*, *Edmontosaurus*, and *Triceratops* rear legs. Which do you think was faster? (Dorothy Sigler Norton)

a hard time being a hunter. But I think he could run fast enough. His legs were longer, and they were built more like runner legs than those of a *Triceratops* or a duckbill. *T. rex* and other running dinosaurs ran on the balls of their feet, raising their heels off the ground. Like an ostrich.

Okay, so even if Stan *could* catch a duckbill, how do we know if he actually *did it*? One piece of evidence seems very strong to me: The Duckbill That Got Away. The Denver Museum has a duckbill with a chunk out of its backbone. A *healed* injury—which means the duckbill was hurt but didn't die from the hurt. The chunk matches the size and shape of a *T. rex* bite—a bite nobody else living at that time could have

A healthy duckbill tail can be seen on the skeleton; *Insets:* the bite mark from the Denver specimen shows where a *T. rex* had a snack! (Ed Gerken, Insets: Peter Larson)

< 118 >

Mystery: Dance to the Death?

In Mongolia, probably the coolest fossil I've ever seen is an exhibit where a *Velociraptor* and *Protoceratops* were killed together, maybe in a sudden sandstorm, *right in the middle of a fight*. They are tangled up together. The *Protoceratops* is biting with its beak-like jaws on the *Velociraptor*'s right hand, and the raptor's hind claw is slicing where the *Protoceratops*'s stomach would have been.

Why were they fighting? Is this clear evidence of a predator catching its prey? Not necessarily. Maybe the *Velociraptor* was hungrily attacking the *Protoceratops*. Or maybe one of them was sneaking up to eat the other's eggs. Or maybe one surprised the other, and it got scared and attacked. It *looks* like a dinner date, but we can't be positive. It could be that one asked the other to dance, and they were both so bad they died of embarrassment.

The dueling dinosaurs. (© psihoyos.com)

made. Maybe Sue did it, when she was still hobbling around on her hurt leg and she wasn't on top of her game.

I like to look at living animals to help me imagine the answer. Living animals usually have good reasons for doing what they do. They're smarter at knowing the reasons than I am at making them up. And here's what the biologists say: there is no big animal alive today that is only a scavenger. Not hyenas, not even vultures, nobody. If you're built big and you're a carnivore, you're designed to kill your food. If there's a dead thing just lying there, of course it gets eaten—even by a lion, who normally kills her dinner. But if there's nothing dead nearby, even scavengers will chase something down and kill it. People have filmed vultures scarfing up baby turtles on their mad dash to the ocean. And hyenas actually kill most of their food. Think about it this way: you're home watching TV and you're hungry. If the fridge has a leftover pizza in it, you eat it. Scavenging is easy. But if you're hungry enough, and there's no food cooked, and Mom's not around to snap your fingers at, even a lazy scavenger like you might cook something for yourself. *If somebody's hungry enough, he or she will do whatever's necessary to eat.*

This is my educated guess: anybody with killer claws and a mouthful of cutting teeth, a super

< 119 >

"Mmm, take-out!" (Bill Brent)

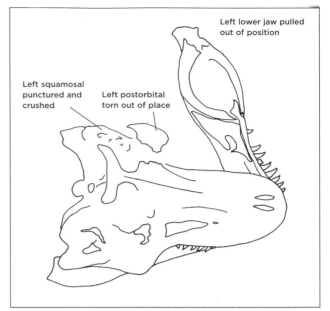

Left lower jaw pulled out of position

Left squamosal punctured and crushed

Left postorbital torn out of place

Sue's battered skull. (Peter Larson)

sniffer, great distance-judging eyeballs, and long legs would be really good at running something down and killing it. But also, I figure that if Sue or Stan were strolling along and suddenly came upon the carcass of a rotting, stinky *Triceratops*, they would eat it. Why not? Free food! No running around. More time for playing Monster Rancher 3.

Murder and Mayhem!

Remember Sue's broken leg? When we find pathologies in bones, they give plenty of clues to a dinosaur's life. Of course, we don't know *how* Sue broke her leg, or *who* may have injured her. But we do know that the pathology became infected, and that it probably didn't heal completely before she died.

Sue also provided the closest thing there is to an actual fact about an ancient event. In the lab, when we finally were able to remove Sue's nose from under her pelvis, we saw something unusual. And interesting. Bones around her left

eye were crushed and punctured or dangled as if by a thread—and the left side of her jaw had been pulled away at the hinge! That is the *evidence*. What does it mean?

Tooth marks on the skull match up with a *T. rex* bite—and just like with the bitten duckbill, no other dinosaur was huge enough to make that bite mark. *I think this was the injury that killed her.*

Because of such strong evidence, I think it's fair to say that Sue was murdered by another *T. rex*. What I can't say is why. Were they fighting over territory? Had someone eaten someone else's lunch? Was someone threatening someone else's children? Did someone say something bad about someone's mother?

I think it's possible that the "other someone" was threatening Sue's children: some of the bones we found of the smaller *T. rex* in Sue's grave had been bitten through. Marks on the bones match the actual *serrations*, or the jagged edges, of *T. rex* teeth.

< 120 >

This lower leg bone (fibula)—which was bitten in half—has tooth mark gouges with serration marks that match a *T. rex* tooth. (Ed Gerken)

Under the microscope, tooth serrations look like a steak knife's. (Neal Larson)

The *T. rex* Steven was preserved with a leg bone, chunks of ribs, and skull parts. All the vertebrae were bitten in half—and their pointy spines were missing. (Peter Larson)

And while we're on the subject of murder, we may as well go a little further than that. We've just discussed the very acceptable idea of *T. rex* innocently walking along a path, finding someone who's already dead, and eating him.

Anybody can understand that. You're very hungry, there's food. You eat it. Well, you do if you're a *T. rex*.

If that something lying in the path is another *T. rex*, we could call that *cannibalism*, which

< 121 >

means eating your own species. Ack. But to me, true cannibalism is saying, "Hmm, I feel like a little *T. rex* sirloin tonight," and going out there and catching a live one. Double ack.

In the field, we've been able to identify the difference between a *T. rex* picnic site and a *Nanotyrannus* site. First of all, both of them left their teeth behind, which is a slam-dunk clue. *Nanotyrannus* was a smaller version of *T. rex*, an animal very similar but a bit different. His mouth was much smaller than *T. rex*'s, and his teeth were narrower and shorter. He was also much more polite. Where *T. rex* destroyed and ate nearly everything, *Nanotyrannus* was neat and tidy. He neatly stripped meat from bones and left the bones whole.

Three *T. rex* I've seen had their vertebrae and ribs bitten through or parts actually gnawed off by another *T. rex*. That's where the cannibal would get the meat we call T-bone and tenderloin steaks. Just from looking at the messy sites, we can tell a *T. rex* did it, but we don't know if it's an Ack or a Double Ack situation. In Sue's case, however, I'm sorry to say that I think we have identified a Double Ack situation. Sue's family was in little pieces beside her in the grave. Heads chopped off, legs snapped. You are what you eat.

CODE WORDS

Binocular vision	Gastroliths
Brain case	Gizzard stones
Cannibal, cannibalism	Mashing teeth
CAT scan	Predator
Cerebrum	Pubis
Cutting teeth	Relative
Depth of field	Scavenger
Ethmoid	Serrations

< 122 >

Developing and Testing a Theory:
The Scientific Guessing Game

Karen Chin studies poop. That's all she does. She's the World's Expert on Fossil Poop, the paleontologist all of us turn to when we have a poop question. She's found burrows of ancient dung beetles in duckbill poop. She's found preserved duckbill dinosaur muscle tissue in *T. rex* poop. Who would have imagined so much information could be found in these kinds of leftovers? Karen is a *specialist*.

So is Kirk Johnson, who is a paleobotanist—a plant guy. When we find fossil leaves or cones at our dig sites, we call Kirk. But sometimes it's hard to find him, because he does as much fieldwork as anyone in paleontology. He's almost always out in the field, looking for fossil plants that existed just before and just after dinosaurs died. To do this, he digs long vertical ditches that span the rocks crossing the dinosaur extinction line. He's discovered and named dozens of new plant species from that time, 65 million years ago.

Bob Bakker, the long-haired paleo wildman you see on *PaleoWorld* and *Bonehead Detectives*, is a *generalist*. He knows lots of things about lots of different dinosaurs, and about living animals. We'll be talking a lot about him in a minute.

When you think about what kind of paleontologist you want to be—generalist or specialist,

Top: Specialist Karen Chin. (Courtesy of Karen Chin) *Middle:* Specialist Kirk Johnson. (Courtesy of Kirk Johnson) *Bottom:* Generalist Bob Bakker. (Peter Larson)

< 123 >

Jen Harvey, iStockphoto

Leah-Ann Thompson, iStockphoto

Kenneth C. Zirkel, iStockphoto

Monika Adamczyk, iStockphoto

Do these look like dinosaurs to you?

or what kind of specialist—you might know right away. Maybe you really love *only* club tails of *Ankylosaurus*, or instead you might want to generally clean up the entire dinosaur classification system.

No matter which you choose, you'll learn how to think like a scientist. You'll use the Hypothesis-Theory-Evidence-Conclusion equation to figure things out.

So far we've talked about dinosaur gender, *Triceratops* elbows, broken bones, kid growth spurts, family life, how a dinosaur stood, teeth, noses, eyes, and brains. We looked at hypotheses and theories and the problems scientists have with agreeing on them. Now's the time to take one idea and follow it from start to finish. Well, as close to "finish" as any scientific idea can get.

< 124 >

Mark Lane, iStockphoto

Greg Wolkins, iStockphoto

From Harter, 1979, *Animals*, p. 85

Kian Khoon Tan, iStockphoto

Characters define who we are.

The Question

Are dinosaurs the direct ancestors of birds?

The Observations

For a long time, scientists have been looking at animals and making observations about their bodies. They noticed that each kind of animal is different from other animals, because of certain parts or features, called *characters*. Fish have gills. Giraffes have long necks. Anteaters have long tongues. Camels have humps. Ducks have webbed feet. Bats have sonar. Get the picture?

Finally they made lists of the parts of each animal that made it special. Everybody knew the characters that made a bird a bird.

What tells us a bird is a bird?

- A bird has a wishbone.
- A bird has feathers.
- A bird has very unusual, fused hands—which form wings—with no claws on its fingers.
- A bird has special wrist joints to fold its wings.
- A bird has a beak, with no teeth.

< 125 >

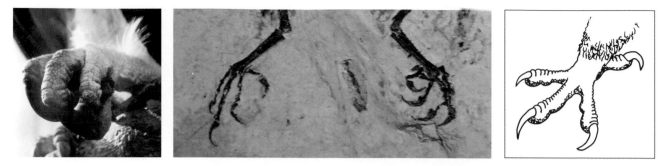

From left to right: An eagle foot with grasping toes; feet from a fossil perching bird, and a drawing of the backward-pointed hallux. These creatures could use their feet for perching or for grabbing victims. (Left: Nat Hagey, iStockphoto; Middle: Peter Larson; Right: Peter Larson)

- Nearly all birds have a backward-pointing big toe, called a hallux. It is usually used for perching, although eagles pick up mice with theirs.

- A bird has a short tail with a *pygostyle*—where tail vertebrae have fused together to form a "rudder" for steering in flight, through air *or* water (think of penguins!).

- A bird's pubis, one of its pelvic bones, is rotated backward.

- A bird has hollow bones.

- A bird is warm-blooded.

No other kind of animal has *all* of these characters. A duckbilled platypus might have a beak, but it has no wings or perching toe or wishbone—or feathers, for that matter. A bat might have wings that fold, but with a different wrist bone. A bat also has no beak or rotated pubis or hollow bones or feathers. It's a flying weasel with a regular weasel-like skeleton

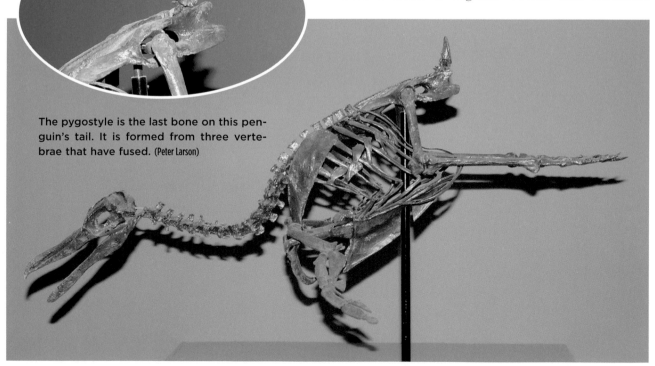

The pygostyle is the last bone on this penguin's tail. It is formed from three vertebrae that have fused. (Peter Larson)

< 126 >

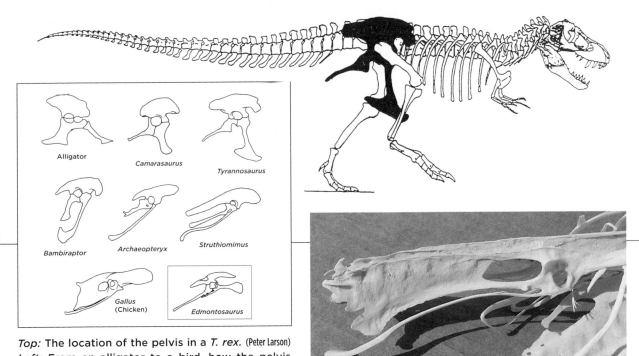

Top: The location of the pelvis in a *T. rex.* (Peter Larson)
Left: From an alligator to a bird, how the pelvis changed through evolution. Compare with the ornithischian pelvis of Edmontosaurus, which is unrelated. (Peter Larson) *Right:* The pelvis of a modern loon. (Peter Larson)

except for really long fingers. You see? It's the whole bird package that makes a bird. A duck-billed platypus is definitely *not* a bird.

There was no question about this, and everybody knew when he or she was looking at a bird. It was simple. Birds were *birds*. Later, in 1824 and 1825, the first dinosaurs were officially described

in scientific papers—but nobody knew they were dinosaurs. They were *Megalosaurus* and *Iguanodon*—and everyone thought they were giant lizards. When this was happening, nobody even *thought* about birds. Birds were birds. Lizards were lizards, even if they were giant. No problem.

Then, eighteen years later, in 1842, Sir

A bat's wings are very different from a bird's wings. (Don Pfritzer, Courtesy of the U.S. Fish and Wildlife Service)

It takes more than a bill to make a duckbilled platypus into a duck. (From Harter, 1979, *Animals*, p. 83)

< 127 >

Richard Owen first made up the word *Dinosauria*, to show that dinosaurs were not lizards, after all. This was a word like "reptile" or "mammal." It meant people had realized there was another kind of creature to get to know. Dinosaurs. But here came the first clue that something was going to happen. Owen noticed some things about these dinosaurs. He said they had a different pelvis and legs from a reptile and *their feet looked like a bird's*. At first, that was okay, because nobody had said only birds could have bird feet.

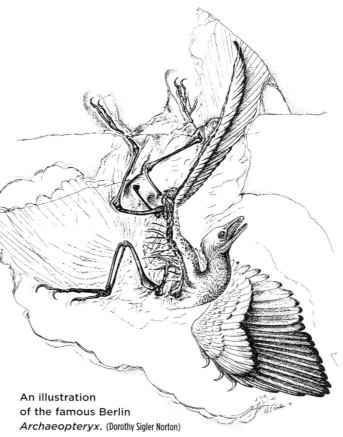

A *T. rex* foot looks like a giant bird foot. (Dorothy Sigler Norton)

Then came the uproar. In 1861, *Archaeopteryx* was discovered. It looked like a bird, but it also looked like a dinosaur.

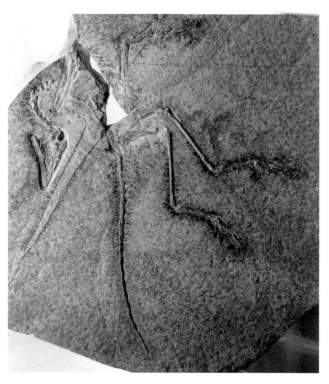

One of the more recent *Archaeopteryx* specimens. (Peter Larson)

Hypothesis #1: Birds descended from dinosaurs

By 1870, many scientists had been looking at *Archaeopteryx*. This weird bird creature caused some scientists to ask, "Were dinosaurs the great-grandparents of birds?" This question started an argument. It also became the first hypothesis about whether birds and dinosaurs came from the same branch of the family tree. *Archaeopteryx* straddled the line between two completely "different" kinds of animals. How it was labeled and identified and categorized would be the first evidence in proving Hypothesis #1.

Was *Archaeopteryx* a dinosaur? Or was he a bird? Or was he a missing link that joined them together as one big, happy family?

An illustration of the famous Berlin *Archaeopteryx*. (Dorothy Sigler Norton)

< 128 >

Birds have:	Archaeopteryx has:	
	Bird characters	**Theropod characters**
Wishbone	Wishbone	
Feathers	Feathers	
Fused hands without claws		Dinosaur hands with claws
Wing-folding wrist joints	Wing-folding wrist joints	
Beak with no teeth		Teeth, but no serrations
Backward pointing toe	Backward pointing toe	
Short tail with pygostyle		Long tail, with no pygostyle
Backward-rotated pubis	Slightly backward-rotated pubis	
Hollow bones	Hollow bones	
Warm-blooded	Probably warm-blooded	

Since *Archaeopteryx* had three theropod characters, everybody looked hard at him. He had a long tail, finger claws, and strange teeth—they looked like dinosaur teeth, but they had no serrations. Weird. Everybody agreed he was a missing link, but to what? Some scientists were very sure that Hypothesis #1 was wrong.

Hypothesis #2: Birds did not descend from dinosaurs, but instead from some other, unknown animal

Most scientists believed that *Archaeopteryx* could not be the missing link to dinosaurs for a very spe-cial reason: evolution. Evolution says that animal species change through time, and eventually change into entire new species. Whether slowly or suddenly, all species today came from other species from the past, and all species are linked together this way. Animal One leads to Animal Two, and then to Animal Three, and so on.

Here's an example. A branch of the horse tree included *Eohippus* (Animal One, a small, four-toed horse). *Eohippus* changed little by little until (Animal Two) *Mesohippus* developed—minus one toe. *Mesohippus* developed into *Parahippus* (Animal Three, a larger three-toed horse, with its middle toe much larger than the others). *Parahippus* changed into today's horse,

< 129 >

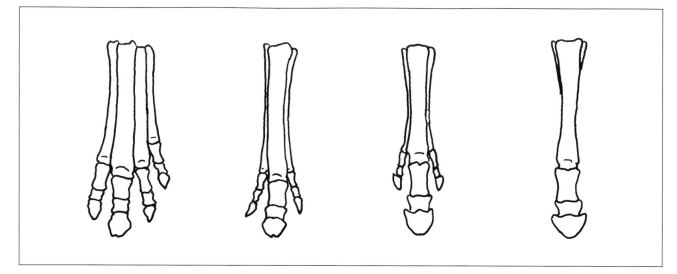

The evolution of the horse's front foot, from left to right: *Eohippus, Mesohippus, Parahippus, Equus.* (Peter Larson)

Once snakes lost their legs, they were gone forever. (Left: U.S. Fish and Wildlife Service; Right: BHI file photo)

Equus (Animal Four, the largest horse with only one "toe"). *Mesohippus* didn't erase *Eohippus*, and *Parahippus* didn't erase *Mesohippus*. They *evolved* into different species, more or less, one after the other.

Evolution also says that Animal One, like a lizard, might have a certain character, like legs. Animal Two, like a snake, loses those legs. Snakes don't need legs, and they actually lose the gene that allows snakes to make legs. Whatever becomes Animal Three after snakes cannot have legs, either—at least not the same kind of legs.

Because of the randomness of evolution, lost legs don't redevelop in the same way in the same line of animals. If snakes someday develop legs, they will look different and be made differently from their ancestor's reptile legs. The odds are a billion to one against any new snake legs—and a billion-billion (that's called a google) against exact-same legs. This is a rule of evolution.

In the Theropod–Bird Hypothesis, scientists knew that reptiles, which have been around longer, led to dinosaurs. Reptiles were Animal One in the chain—and reptiles had collar-

< 130 >

Mystery: The Evolution of Evolution

Science: In 1859, Charles Darwin came up with the basic ideas of evolution, but he wasn't the only one who ever talked about how animals lined up after one another on the family tree. Stephen Jay Gould and Niles Eldredge also did it, and they found that the fossil record wasn't as neat and tidy as Darwin thought it would be.

Darwin said that life evolved from one animal to the next through time, in small, smooth steps. Other paleontologists found that while sometimes animals evolved gradually, other times changes happened quickly. In fact, sometimes a descendant lived *at the same time* as its ancestor.

The fossil record also showed several times in geologic history where big chunks of animal and plant life on Earth just stopped—and new, different life began. (See Appendix B for the geologic extinction timeline.) The geologic ages, like the Cretaceous and the Jurassic, are defined based on these sudden changes, which are called "extinction events." Scientists thought extinctions occurred because of natural disasters or other global changes in ecology. Each time lots of animals died, there was room for new animals to develop. Extinction is probably one of the biggest driving forces of evolution.

Religion: Many scientists think evolution occurred on its own, as a natural, scientific event. But every culture has a different sort of story about the creation of the earth and all its life. No matter what the culture, its creation story includes a higher being—called God, Mother Earth, Allah, or the Great Spirit, among others.

Some creation stories say that all living things were created individually by the supernatural force. Other stories say that the creator may have started life and helped it along, intentionally causing an evolutionary process to occur.

Whether a creator or a Big Bang helped get the ball of life rolling, people have been trying to explain the great mystery of life for as long as they have had the thinking and feeling parts of their brains. What do you think?

bones. Animal Two, dinosaurs, had no collarbones or wishbones, or anything that could have turned into a wishbone. Since birds for sure had wishbones, scientists knew *birds could not be Animal Three* in the dinosaur chain. Wishbones are actually collarbones that fused together, so scientists figured birds had to get their wishbones from somewhere else. From somebody else's collarbones. This meant birds were Animal Three on some *other* chain—but nobody knew which one.

That was Hypothesis #2: Birds did not come from dinosaurs. They came from somewhere else, but we don't know where.

Everybody felt pretty good about Hypothesis #2, because they also knew that dinosaurs also had no feathers or backward-facing hallux or folding wrist.

< 131 >

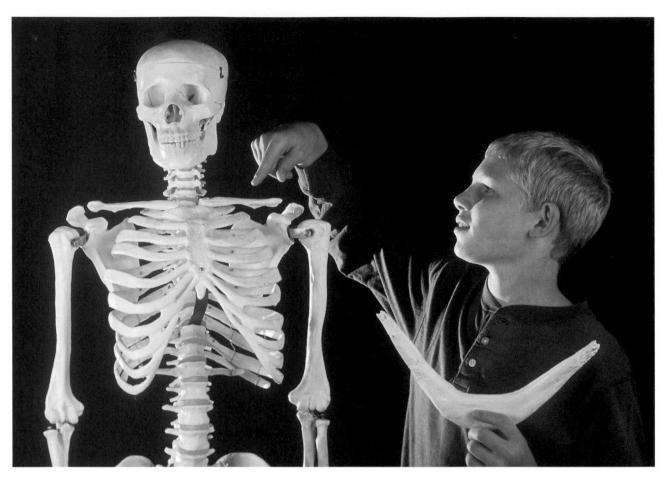

Wishbones are fused collarbones. (Layne Kennedy)

When birds have teeth, the teeth are smooth—with no serrations. Compare the serrated *Nanotyrannus* tooth (*left*) with the smooth teeth from the Cretaceous bird *Ichthyornis.* (*right*) (Neal Larson)

But what about *Archaeopteryx*? What about his dinosaur characters?

Well, scientists simply changed the definition of a bird to include those three dinosaur possibilities. They decided that a bird might have a long tail, finger claws, and teeth without making it something else. They also paid attention to the teeth: they decided that if a particular bird *did* have teeth, its teeth would have no serrations. This was another thing that made them different from dinosaurs.

< 132 >

So Hypothesis #2 actually changed what a bird is:

NOW what tells us a bird is a bird?
- A bird has a wishbone.
- A bird has feathers.
- A bird has special wrist joints to fold its wings.
- A bird has a beak (with or without teeth).
- Many birds have a backward-pointing big toe, called a hallux.
- A bird's pubis is rotated backward.
- A bird has hollow bones.
- A bird is warm-blooded.
- A toothed bird has no serrations on its teeth.

Phew. Everyone was glad *that* was over. And this settled the bird-dinosaur problem for more than one hundred years.

Then things really got exciting.

Hypothesis #1 — The Sequel: Birds did too descend from dinosaurs

In 1966, Bob Bakker was in college. He's the wildest and craziest of all paleontologists, and he always has fresh ideas. This fresh idea just popped out of his cerebrum all by itself: he decided dinosaurs had to be warm-blooded. Once he made that crucial connection, *everything about dinosaurs changed*. Bob drew pictures of leaping dinosaurs, dancing dinosaurs, dinosaurs with claws in full-on attack position, and with bloody grins on their faces—even dinosaurs with feathers. No more of that business about slow-moving reptiles lurking in swamps!

This was Bob Bakker's first drawing of feathered dinosaurs, two fighting *Deinonychus*, which he drew in 1973. (Dr. Robert Bakker)

< 133 >

A bat's wing is made mostly of spread-out fingers; a bird's fingers are fused together. You can see the difference in these 50-million-year-old fossils, which came from the Green River Formation in Wyoming. The bat is on the left. (Top: From Richardson et al., circa 1860, The Museum of Natural History, Mammalia plate 5; Bottom: Peter Larson)

Okay, the idea wasn't just out of the blue. First, Bob looked at history. "For big animals, it's better to be warm-blooded," he remembers thinking at the time. "If you want to be big, anywhere on the earth, you don't have anyplace to hide from danger. You can't back down your burrow, or climb a tree. You're just too big. All you can do is fight or run away, and it's easier to do either of those if you're warm-blooded." He thought of giant tortoises, and just imagined how well they can fight or run away, compared to, well, a lion or an elephant—or you.

Second, he looked at biology. "Dinosaur legs, both front and back, were designed for continuous and fast running," he says. "A *Brontosaurus*'s front legs do not look like a tortoise's."

And with those thoughts running through his head, Bob wrote a scientific paper that was published in 1968. It was called, "The Superiority of Dinosaurs."

< 134 >

Around the same time, Bob's professor at Yale, John Ostrom, was working on one of the raptors, *Deinonychus*, when he noticed a couple of amazing characters. Everybody knew that *Deinonychus* was a dinosaur, but Ostrom was looking at wing-folding bird wrists, and a backward-pointing pubis bone, and halluxes that pointed to the side. Not quite to the back, but certainly not to the front! What was the deal?

Instead of a bird with theropod parts—like *Archaeopteryx*—*Deinonychus* was a dinosaur with bird parts!

Flying creatures need very special adaptations for their wings to function. For bats, their long fingers fold up their wings. For birds, a special, one-of-a-kind wrist joint allows the wings to fold. It is a *specialized* character, something necessary for a bird to function as a bird. Nobody else besides birds had ever had that wrist joint—except *Deinonychus*. So Ostrom thought it was especially *birdlike*. The other characters, the pubis and hallux, also were birdlike, but the wrist was especially important. A few years later, Ostrom published a paper called, "The Ancestry of Birds."

By now, both Bob and Ostrom had looked back at old Hypothesis #1 and said that birds and theropod dinosaurs *were* related after all. They thought birds actually had come from the theropod branch of the family tree—even if dinosaurs had no wishbones or feathers.

More Evidence

China has the best fossil bird sites of the right age to help prove or disprove Hypothesis #1— The Sequel. The sediments there preserve a point in time after *Archaeopteryx*, but way before dinosaurs became extinct.

A wonderful location in China is an ancient lake north of present-day Beijing that existed about 120 million years ago and almost certainly was formed because of active volcanoes in that area. The lake's sediment was very fine, and these millions of years later, it comes apart into sheets, like playing cards. The lake preserved the most delicate details of these fabulous bird fossils—including some of the oldest actual bird feathers ever. Not just imprints, or suggestions of feathers, but actual Type I fossil feathers.

Many kinds of birds were found in that lake, and they had a variety of characters. Of course, they all had the basic bird features, like wishbones and backward hallux and backward pubis. They had folding wrists and hollow bones. But other characters were mixed, depending on which bird you picked up.

Some had teeth and feathers, but no claws.
Some had teeth and claws, but no feathers.
Some had feathers, but no teeth or claws.

One species of bird, *Confuciusornus*, had claws and feathers, but no teeth. More than a thousand *Confuciusornus* have been found in the lake, all in one layer. Scientists think maybe a whole flock was killed by a volcanic eruption.

All of these birds were more birdy than *Archaeopteryx*, but less birdy than today's birds. They were important because they showed how birds changed along their evolutionary chain. They also showed how flexible the "bird definition" was.

At first, scientists just thought this was interesting in the bird-only way. This bird and that bird. "Hmm, very interesting," they said.

Confuciusornus santus, a 122-million-year-old fossil bird from Lioning, China. (Layne Kennedy)

< 136 >

Then something messed them up totally.

Scientists found some dinosaurs with *wishbones*.

Gulp.

Bambi

The Linster family—complete with seven kids—had been leasing and digging a Montana dinosaur quarry for six years when something exciting happened. For the exciting thing to be able to happen, those six years of finding mixed-up duckbills and whole duckbills, along with bits and pieces of theropods, had to happen first. All the Linsters, even the little ones, were excellent, self-trained, amateur paleontologists, and they were mapping the quarry and carefully counting the bones and taking notes. They had plenty of experience, and good eyes.

The exciting thing happened to kid number four, Wes, who was thirteen in 1993. On Labor Day weekend, he happened to be digging at the quarry by himself when he turned over a chunk of dirt. He saw a tiny jaw bone with tiny meat-eater teeth in it. Many people might not even have noticed it, but Wes knew he had something great—he just didn't know what. Everybody helped find more of the dinosaur. Then they plastered blocks of bones into field jackets and took them home. Together, the family carefully removed most of the matrix, and ended up with many bones from this little creature—a little creature that looked like an adorable, horrible, teeny-tiny *Velociraptor*.

The Linsters had met paleontologist Dave Burnham, who went to look at the find. The first bone he saw was the wishbone. In dinosaurs, wishbones are called *furculas*. Not only did this

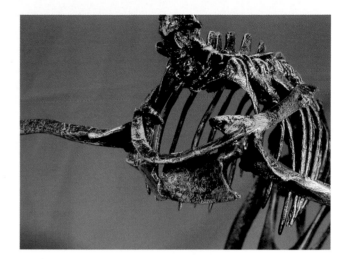

Bambiraptor has a birdlike wishbone. (Larry Shaffer)

creature *have* a wishbone, but also it looked *just like Archaeopteryx's*, kind of like a boomerang.

After 7,000 hours of work, Dave also found the skull parts—some of which were as small as your fingernail, and just as thin. He worked slowly and carefully under a microscope. He had to be extra careful, because the whole skull was only five inches long and the whole thing could fit in your hand. It was so little, Dave called it Bambi. All together, Bambi measured 33 inches long—just a little shorter than a yardstick. His wingspan stretched only two feet—a little bigger than a chicken's, but smaller than an eagle.

It turned out that young Wes had found one of the most important dinosaurs ever. *Bambiraptor* was a whole new species, something no one had ever seen before. Relative to body size, he has the biggest dinosaur breast bone yet, a *sternum*—similar to a bird's—which very few dinosaurs have. He has the special birdlike, wing-folding wrists, too. But *Bambiraptor* is mostly a dinosaur, with a dinosaur skull, dinosaur serrated teeth, dinosaur feet and hands that look kind of like

< 137 >

Bambiraptor was even cooler than *Velociraptor!* (Peter Larson)

Surely feathers, not a spotted furry coat, adorned *Bambiraptor's* muscular body. (Pat Redman, From *The University of Kansas Paleontological Contributions, new series,* courtesy of and © 2000, The University of Kansas, Paleontological Institute)

Archaeopteryx's, and razor-sharp killing claws on his feet. Bambi truly is one of the most birdlike dinosaurs. Dave calls him, "a running, killing machine with long arms."

Bambi's also very smart. He is a cousin of *Velociraptor* and—remember?—so far these raptors had the smartest dinosaur brains. When you compare the raptors' brains with their body sizes, Bambi's brain is the largest of all. His brain's thinking part—the cerebrum—is huge. His smelling part is tiny, like today's birds. This was a bird who could think on his feet!

And he had a wishbone.

Wishbone? WISHBONE?

"DINOSAURS DON'T HAVE WISH-BONES!" everybody shouted.

But they did. The first one was found in *Oviraptor* in the 1980s. Then several other theropod wishbones came to light in the 1990s. *Bambiraptor, Velociraptor, Albertosaurus, Gorgosaurus,* and *Allosaurus* all had them. The first *T. rex* wishbone was found in 2001 when we dug Bucky.

The more wishbones we found, the more we were able to see how that bone changed over time. *Bambiraptor's Archaeopteryx*-like, flattened wishbone was the more "primitive" version. Bambi's cousins, *Velociraptor* and *Oviraptor,* both have "advanced" wishbones that look more adapted for flight! They are shaped more like a modern bird's, and include that part that sticks up in the middle, called a hypocladium.

< 138 >

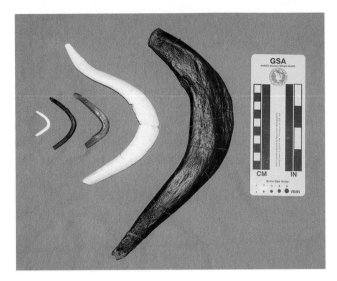

Dinosaur wishbones! *T. rex*'s is on the right. (Peter Larson)

Recent and fossil feathers are virtually identical. (Peter Larson)

And as if all this wishbone business wasn't bad enough, then the bird definition got *another* hit. Scientists found a dinosaur with *downy feathers*. These are the soft "under feathers" that baby birds have when they hatch, and adult birds use as insulation. Not the kind of feathers birds use to fly—those are called *flight feathers*. The dinosaur who had the downy feathers was called *Sinosauropteryx*, and he had all theropod characters—except for those confusing downy feathers.

The paleontologists who did not agree with Theropod-Bird Hypothesis #1—The Sequel, said, "Those aren't *real* feathers! Those aren't *flight* feathers! Those are fuzz. DINO FUZZ! They don't count."

Then, back in that same Chinese fossil lake, scientists found the last pieces of evidence that would change the bird definition forever. They found *Caudipteryx* and seven more meat-eating dinosaurs, many of which haven't even been named yet. Many of these were like *Deinonychus*, but feathers were found preserved on their

bodies. Flight feathers. Real, actual bird flying feathers on real, honest-to-goodness theropod dinosaurs. No one could ever again say that only birds had feathers. So, were these flying dinosaurs? Did *Deinonychus* have feathers that just haven't been found yet? Was everybody a bird? Was everybody a dinosaur? *What was a bird anyway?*

Meanwhile, Mark Norell at New York's American Museum of Natural History had been to Mongolia. There he found *Mononykus*, a creature that some scientists believe was a bird, and some believe was a dinosaur. He also found many kinds of oviraptor relatives, and another one was found in South Dakota. At least two of these, along with China's *Caudipteryx*, had a short bird tail! The kind with the pygostyle that helps birds steer when they're flying. Plus, the *Oviraptors* also had wishbones.

And more theropods, including *T. rex*, were found with the sideways-facing—and even somewhat backward—big toe, the perching hallux. As more species and more good speci-

< 139 >

mens were found, scientists could watch the hallux evolution happen right before their very eyes. As dinosaurs developed, the hallux moved from the front to the side—and sometimes all the way to the back. Why do you think theropod halluxes started moving? Did the little dinos perch in trees? What were they holding onto?

This Hypothesis #1 — The Sequel was exhausting. More WISHBONES! Feathers! Rudder tails! Perching toes! Things were changing so fast, it was hard to keep track.

Then, in 2003, came *Microraptor*. He was the weirdest of all. He was definitely not a bird, although he had some bird characters. But can you imagine? He had flight feathers— flight feathers that did something nobody else's feathers have ever done. They went all down his arms *and legs*, and even onto his feet! Some people called him the "four-winged dinosaur."

That sounds silly, having four wings, but with so many feathers, he definitely made a point. It was just like he was screaming: "HEY, dinosaurs CAN TOO have feathers! Looky here!"

The Theory

Okay. Let's think about all of this for a minute.

The second bird definition said:

NOW what tells us a bird is a bird?
- A bird has a wishbone.
- A bird has feathers.
- A bird has special wrist joints to fold its wings.

< 140 >

- A bird has a beak (with or without teeth).
- Many birds have a backward-pointing big toe, called a hallux.
- A bird's pubis is rotated backward.
- A bird has hollow bones.
- A bird is warm-blooded.
- A toothed bird has no serrations on its teeth.

After theropods were found with wishbones, feathers, bird wrists, halluxes, and backward-rotated pubises, this left the bird definition with fewer bird-only characters.

AFTER ALL THIS,
what tells us a bird is a bird?
- A bird has a beak.
- A bird has hollow bones.
- A bird is warm-blooded.
- A toothed bird has no serrations on its teeth.

Most of the original bird-only definition is destroyed by all these birdy dinosaurs. With all this evidence, most scientists have come to believe that Hypothesis #1—The Sequel is correct. The idea that theropods are the ancestors of birds is now an Accepted Theory. It's almost a fact, like Earth being round. But we're not quite as sure about The Theory as we are about the Earth. After all, we can *see* that Earth is round.

Not *everybody* is convinced. Because paleontologists are paleontologists, a few still believe that the similarities between birds and theropods do *not* mean that one *descended* from the other.

They say "birds are birds," and "theropods are theropods." The fact that they are similar is just because they are similar. They say it doesn't mean birds and theropods are *related*.

What do you think? *How do we really decide which is which?*

Let's take one last look at the rest of the bird definition. The truth is, almost all bird-only characters have been slaughtered by birdy dinosaurs. These last few just got overshadowed by the feathers and wishbones.

Juggling ancient bird–dinosaurs *Archaeopteryx*, *Confuciusornis*, and *Bambiraptor*. (Dorothy Sigler Norton)

< 141 >

Beaks: We're not sure if any dinosaurs had them, but some probably did. Bird beaks, which are made of keratin—like our hair—usually do not preserve as fossils, because they disappear like skin and guts. But we know that bird beaks are supported by bones in the skull. Bones that have a very specific texture. Theropods called *Gallimimus*, *Struthiomimus*, and *Ornithomimus* have the same texture of bone, right on the face where a beak would attach. Plus, they have no teeth! We'll have to look very carefully at future discoveries of these "bird-mimic" dinosaurs.

Tooth serrations: A few theropods have crossed over to the bird side of the definition. Dinosaurs like *Spinosaurus* and *Paronychodon*, who are not even closely related to each other, have smooth teeth with no dinosaurlike serrations at all.

Hollow bones: This is an easy one. *All* theropods have hollow bones. *T. rex* and *Allosaurus* and *Velociraptor* and *Carnotaurus* and *Megalosaurus* and *Oviraptor* and *Carcharodontosaurus* and all the others have hollow spaces in their skulls and vertebrae. Scientists think one reason a theropod like *T. rex* would have hollow bones is for balancing its gigantic, powerful, heavy skull. The front of the body lightened up, and the tail vertebrae remained solid—all to keep Stan from doing a face plant.

Warm-blooded: Well. As more and more birdy characters were found in some dinosaurs, nearly every scientist agreed with Hypothesis #1—The Sequel. They realized that there was no way theropods could be cold-blooded like their reptile ancestors. They just couldn't. One major piece of evidence was the feathers. Downy or flight feathers acted as insulation to hold in body heat. This was an outfit no self-

Many dinosaurs must have been as energetic as living birds are today. (Dean E. Biggins, Courtesy of U.S. Fish and Wildlife Service)

respecting, cold-blooded reptile would be caught dead in.

Birdlike theropod characters were knocking reptile characters flat. The original, boring reputation of slow, damp, dumb theropod dinosaurs had to go. This is the part when we leave the fossil record and dive right into Big Ideas. Big Ideas in our own heads.

Possible Conclusions

Bob Bakker was the first one to jump on the warm-blooded dinosaur bandwagon. He drew dinosaurs with feathers *decades* before fossils proving him right were found. But as birdy dinosaurs popped up like crazy, more scientists agreed with his bird models. Everyone started to imagine dinosaurs that acted like birds. Lively! Energetic! Busy!

Bob's enthusiasm, along with supporting fossil evidence, made dinosaurs even more exciting. It's *exciting* to imagine raptors racing around, double-teaming a duckbill for the lunch menu. Bob's ideas sent all kinds of scientists packing out to the field—in search of dinosaurs. The search was amazing. The search was productive. That's why so many more creatures have been found. More of the ones we already knew and brand new kinds that we didn't even know about. It's a great time to become a paleontologist!

This new image of dinosaurs is also why more and more information has been uncovered—leading to more and more Big Ideas. See what you think of these. They take us from bones we can see into bodies we can only imagine.

Big Idea #1: Breathing

Remember the hollow bones we were talking about before? You might think that the bones are hollow tubes, like drinking straws. But that's not what "hollow" means when it comes to birds and dinosaurs. It means the bones have pockets that are connected by little passageways—like honeycombs. Birds are the only *living* creatures to have this system, and it's just like the system we see in the bones of theropods, sauropods, and pterosaurs (flying reptiles).

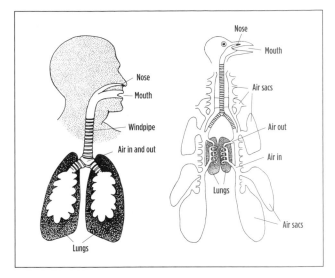

People and birds (and some dinosaurs!) breathe very differently. (Dorothy Sigler Norton)

We think it has two functions. One is to be lighter. If you're a theropod, you want to be lighter for balancing. If you're a bird, you want to be lighter for flying—which might be a kind of happy accident. Because the main function, whether you're a bird *or* a dinosaur, has to do with breathing.

Mystery: How Breathing Works

Among other jobs, blood takes oxygen through the body and delivers it to the hard-working muscles and organs. This is true in anybody's body. A bird body or a person's body or a turtle's body. When air goes into lungs, the oxygen seeps through tiny holes in blood vessels and is grabbed up and carried away by red blood cells. When we're done with air, much of what's left is carbon dioxide, which is like our "exhaust." The carbon dioxide is dumped by those red blood cells back into the lungs where it can get breathed out.

The size of the heart muscle is important, too. If it's bigger and stronger, it pushes more oxygen through our bodies faster. In relationship to their bodies, birds have much larger hearts than we do—from one and one-half to two times bigger! This means more blood with all that super-charged oxygen is zooming through their bodies with less effort. No wonder they can fly at 30,000 feet—where we need *an airplane* and extra oxygen to survive.

< 143 >

Bones for breathing? I know, it's totally weird. First let's look at how *we* breathe.

All mammals, reptiles, and amphibians have lungs like balloons. We breathe into the balloon, and the oxygen gets soaked up into our blood. Then the used air gets breathed back out the same opening—our mouth and nose. The problem with our balloon system is that we never get rid of all the used air. We keep mixing fresh air with our already-used air, and it's just not very efficient. We could never fly because these lungs just can't deliver enough oxygen to fuel wing muscles.

Birds are much better breathing machines. A bird's lungs have openings on *both* ends, and *air sacs* in front of and behind their lungs. The air sacs, not the lungs, act like balloons, inflating and deflating. They pump the air through the lungs and out a different pipe than it went in. It's like a Hot Wheels track. All one way. The fresh air never runs into the old, used air. No used air hangs around anywhere. It's because of these air sacs that the bones have hollow spaces. The air sacs kind of pushed their way into the bones as the bones grew. Wherever air sacs need to be, the bones have made room by leaving either actual holes or cups.

So why do we see pockets and hollows in the bones of some dinosaurs? Why would theropods, sauropods, and pterosaurs need this supercharged breathing system?

It makes sense that a pterosaur would have them. You know pterosaurs—those flying dinosaurlike creatures. They have their own, separate spot on the family tree—because their ankles and wrists are different, and their wings are formed in a totally different way. But still. They *flew*. Pterosaurs would need the fancy breathing system to fly. And their bones show the honeycomb from air sacs.

T. rex vertebrae are riddled with holes, and their insides look like a honeycomb. (Peter Larson)

< 144 >

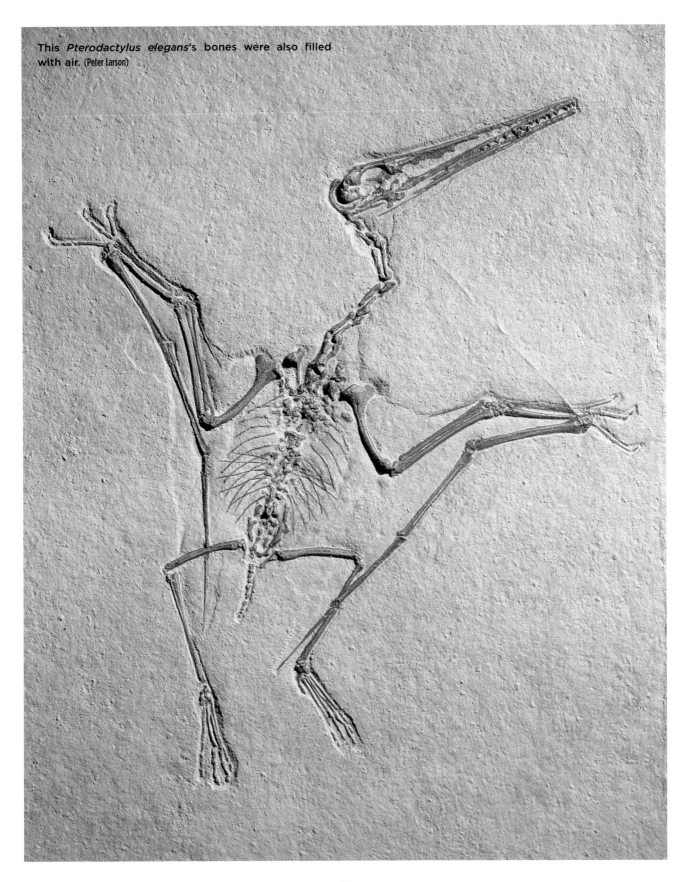

This *Pterodactylus elegans*'s bones were also filled with air. (Peter Larson)

< 145 >

We think that long-necked sauropods had to have the system because their necks were too long for air to even *reach* their lungs on the first breath. Bob Bakker has said that without efficient lungs and heart, long-necks would have had trouble with their blood pressure. If they lowered their heads too fast, their heads might have blown right off their necks!

But why would theropods need the bird breathing system? They needed to run faster—to keep everyone else on the menu.

Big Idea #2: Eggs

Do you think egg-laying is a character? Let's think about who lays hard-shelled eggs: birds, some reptiles, and dinosaurs. While we can't *watch* Sue lay eggs, we can compare both her body and her nest to living animals.

The first thing is how everybody's body works. Eggs pass through tubes called *oviducts*. In crocodiles, many eggs line up at one time in the two oviducts until they're fertilized. Then the croc lays them all at once and covers them to keep heat in and sun, rain, and varmints out. In a bird, only one oviduct works, and only one egg is formed per day. Whereas a croc can lay 80 to 100 eggs in one sitting, a bird takes several days to lay several eggs. Almost all birds incubate their eggs by sitting on them. Crocodiles don't sit on their nests, but they may guard them like crazy.

Over the last ten years, we've found lots of dinosaur eggs, nests, and even embryos—some inside the eggs, and some just hatching. Theropod nests look like giant bowls with rims—just like a crocodile's. Since we know how crocodiles make their nests—by kicking, kicking, kicking—we can just imagine a *T. rex* scooping out dirt with its feet, and hunkering down to lay eggs.

Theropod eggs are not round like turtle eggs—or eggs from vegetarian dinosaurs. They are shaped like a fat loaf of French bread, and the largest ones are as big as that. Definitely closer to a football than a golf ball! But there's something completely different about theropod nests: the eggs aren't just plopped in there. They are laid in a circle, pushed into the dirt, and in pairs. *No other creatures lay their eggs in pairs.* Not ever. Not extinct animals, and not living animals.

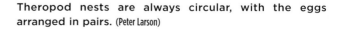

Theropod nests are always circular, with the eggs arranged in pairs. (Peter Larson)

< 146 >

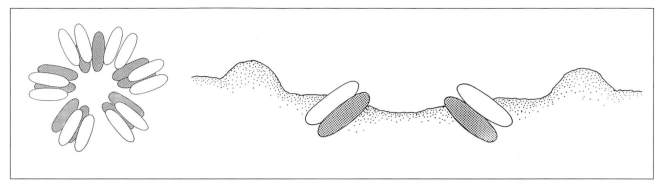

Typical theropod nests from above and from the side. (Dorothy Sigler Norton)

What could this mean? Does it matter? Everything matters!

It means theropods had two oviduct tubes, like a crocodile. Probably the eggs were lined up and fertilized all at once, and then laid in circles in the nests—all in one sitting, two by two by two. It would be hard to stop in the middle of this process and then come back to finish your circle. Imagine stepping into a half-full nest, glancing around your giant legs, and trying to point your bottom the right way.

The pairing shows that the mom theropod actually pushed the eggs down into the ground, instead of just dropping them. Otherwise they would have rolled around, out of position. It also shows that she "fired out of both barrels" at once. That's the part that no other animal has ever done. Why would she do this but nobody else?

Although we've been talking about all the birdlike characters of theropods, this is obviously *not* a birdlike situation. If birds' ancestors used both oviducts at once, why would birds use only one? And why would they create only one egg per day? Why would their bodies have changed through evolution? Some people think a bird's whole laying system changed so a bird

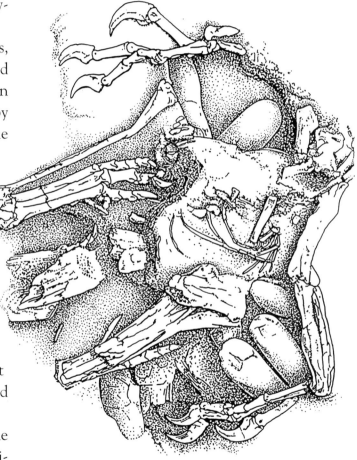

This *Oviraptor* perished while incubating its eggs. (Dorothy Sigler Norton)

wouldn't have a bellyful of heavy eggs in case it had to fly away from danger. Can you think of another reason?

< 147 >

Robins and *T. rex* are closer relatives than you might think! (Michael Skrepnik)

We don't know for sure what happened after Sue's eggs were laid. Other theropods, like *Oviraptor*, sat on their nests like birds. We know that because Mark Norell and Phil Currie found them that way. Probably buried by a sand storm with their little arms wrapped around their eggs.

We also don't know what kind of parent Sue might have been, but we can see how crocodiles and birds act. And with more and more fossils being found each year, soon there may be more evidence to tell us. Babies and teenagers and parents all caught together, playing Terminal Tag with a *Triceratops*.

It sure seems that dinosaurs are not extinct. *Most* of them are, especially the big ones. But not all. It sure seems that plenty of them are flying around at your house right this minute.

Why Did Everyone Else Die?

If birds are the descendants of theropods, and if birds already existed before all other dinosaurs became extinct, why didn't birds become extinct, too? Why did other dinosaurs become extinct? Why didn't *everyone* become extinct?

Dinosaur extinction has caused plenty of arguments in paleontology. Over one hundred ideas and hypotheses have been discussed. Some of them were impossible to prove, like what if strange, new plants didn't agree with dinosaur guts—and all the dinosaurs filled with gas and blew up. Yuck! The fossil record wouldn't really show something like that, would it?

Another idea was that mammals ate all the dinosaur eggs. That's another one that's hard to prove, but we can say that so far no mammal has been found in a dinosaur nest. No dinosaur

Most scientists think that a visitor from outer space, an asteroid, destroyed *T. rex*'s world. (Dorothy Sigler Norton)

eggs—drained of their contents—have been found with mammal teeth marks. It's not impossible, but so far, no evidence. If we did find evidence like this, can you imagine what would have caused those mammals to suddenly change their diets to dinosaur eggs only?

There's one hypothesis that many scientists think has the most evidence. It would explain why everybody who weighed more than one hundred pounds died. The Chicxulub (pronounced *CHICK-sha-lube*) crater is half in and half out of the Gulf of Mexico, in the Yucatan Peninsula. It's 110 miles across, and would have been formed when an asteroid collided with Earth. (See Appendix B for the geologic extinction timeline.) This means a six-mile-wide Cosmic Cannonball plowed into Earth at

40,000 miles per hour, driving seven or eight miles deep into the Earth's crust. It was so big that when it first touched down, its nose was in the dirt, and its rear end was still out in space—outside our atmosphere.

The impact turned the Cannonball into pure energy and spit out all kinds of heat, molten rock, dust, and debris. Scientists have found debris splattered from Mexico to Texas to Haiti to Cuba, and preserved asteroid dust all over what were then all the oceans and on what was then the land in North America. The explosion would have been *50 billion times* larger than the atomic bomb that destroyed Hiroshima, Japan, during World War II.

After such a tremendous blast, the sky was black with smoke and dust, and the sun didn't

< 149 >

reach the earth for perhaps a year or more. There were earthquakes and forest fires, acid rain and giant tsunamis (soo-NA-meez), which are tidal waves. Plants died, plant-eaters died, and then predators died. We think that the only creatures that could live through this were animals that didn't have to eat very often, like crocs, or small creatures who could find shelter and live off dried plants, buried roots, and the carcasses of everybody else—like small mammals and birds.

When everything calmed down again, and the sun came back out, and plants began to grow, there were no large dinosaurs left. This allowed mammals to grow larger than rats and cats—which were as large as mammals got during the 160-million-year reign of the dinosaurs. This made room for us.

CODE WORDS

Air sacs	Hallux
Archaeopteryx	Hypocladium
Asteroid	Inhale
Carbon dioxide	Oviduct
Character	Oxygen
Cold-blooded	Pterosaur
Dinosauria	Pygostyle
Evolution	Specialist
Exhale	Sternum
Extinction events	Tsunami
Furcula	Warm-blooded
Generalist	Wishbone

< 150 >

Your Future Job

Bucky Derflinger is a rodeo cowboy and a rancher. He's a cattle rancher and a dinosaur rancher. Bucky found his first rooted, "whole banana" *T. rex* tooth when he was eight. Some of the dinosaur's bones were there in the ground, next to its tooth. At that time, Bucky didn't know how to look at a fossil site, or how to collect fossils. He didn't even realize what the bones were until years later, but he knew exactly what the tooth was. "Everybody knows a tooth that big around is a *T. rex* tooth!"

Bucky's first bronc ride. (Courtesy of Bucky Derflinger)

He lived with his family out on the prairie of South Dakota, and he looked for bones all the time. His dad and uncle would go bone hunting with him, and they helped him learn about the sediments where they lived. But sometimes, when he was supposed to be helping with chores, like moving cows, Bucky would be distracted, scanning for bones. "Get your eyes up off the ground, son!" his dad would holler. "Don't forget we're working!"

Bucky read everything about dinosaurs he could get his hands on. He got books from the library that told him the names of the different species and what they may have looked like. But he couldn't find anything that helped him learn how to *collect* bones. Most of the time, he collected only what was on the surface—digging where he lived was almost impossible without help, and glue. Most bones he was finding were too crumbly and broken to save. But still, he found plenty of toe bones and other small parts of duckbills and *Triceratops*.

He also got hooked on microsites. "They help train your eye," he says.

< 151 >

Bucky next to his historical find. (Peter Larson)

Jami rides her horse, Cricket, to the dinosaur site her father found. (The Toad)

"You might have five people looking, noses in the dirt, and nobody sees anything at first. Then, suddenly *there they are*, teeth or little bones."

All this eye training paid off. When he was sixteen, Bucky found a deposit of maybe 1,000 fossilized sequoia cones—600 of which he picked up in one day. He also found his second skeleton, a duckbill. Then, when he was twenty, he found two *T. rex* within two months of each other. The first was named Bucky—the teenaged *T. rex* we talked about before. The second might be part of the first *T. rex* that was ever known. Only a couple of vertebrae from that one, found in 1892 by the famous paleontologist E.D. Cope, were collected for a scientific description. The rest was never dug. Pretty

soon we're going to run some chemical analysis tests to see if we can tell for sure if it's the exact same dinosaur.

Either way, we know that Bucky Derflinger has made history with his *T. rex* discoveries. He tied the Sacrison record of finding two *T. rex*. He may have left one in the ground when he was eight, which would have made three. But now Bucky says he's spotted a for-sure number three *T. rex*! This time he definitely knows what to do. He's been working with the professional collectors in our company, and now his fossils are finding homes in museums.

"People need to learn how to collect," Bucky says. "Get in touch with a museum, or someone else who knows what they're doing. Someone

< 152 >

School kids coming to one of our digs. (Ed Gerkin)

who's collected for a long time." That's the only way fossils will be able to tell you their stories.

Now, Bucky shares his favorite pastime—and his stories—with his daughter, Jami. She's been fossil hunting with him since she was two, and now, at seven, she's found lots of fossils, especially croc teeth. "I *love* looking for dinosaur bones," Jami says.

It's a good thing Jami has a mentor. And it's a good thing Bucky has a collecting partner. "I'll be doing this forever, as long as I have eyesight," he says. "I'll crawl through the hills if I have to."

Help!

You've learned how science works. You know how everyone tosses around ideas and hypotheses and then argues about them. Well, there are many questions in paleontology that have not been answered, and we need your help.

Part of what we need is more people like Bucky, who will never stop looking for fossils.

Part of what we need is more expert diggers, and expert preparators—so we can see the evidence clearly.

And part of what we need is more thinking. New ways to think about old problems. Someone new to think up new problems. *New ideas all around.*

< 153 >

Terry Wentz doing what he does best. (Layne Kennedy)

< 154 >

Most of all, we need lots of open minds. Minds that think on their own but still listen to other minds. Bucky says that after he learned a new way to break a colt, he didn't just change over to the new way and throw his old way in the trash. He combined his old way *and* the new way. "It would be wrong for me to break a colt just like that other guy, because I'm not that guy," he says. "I'm different from everybody else, but it doesn't mean I know everything."

No one will break a colt just like Bucky does. No one will study a fossil just like you do. No one.

Here are some examples of paleontologists who learned to look at fossils, or fossil problems, or fossil questions in brand new ways. Their very own, special ways. See if something they're doing gives you ideas about what you want to do. All you need is a Big Idea.

The Big Bite

Greg Erickson was working at the Museum of the Rockies in Montana when he saw a *Triceratops* pelvis with poke holes in it. The holes matched *T. rex* teeth. He wondered how hard the *T. rex* had to bite to get his teeth to go through the bone.

Then Greg wondered, "Can I find out?"

He knew he couldn't use an actual fossil tooth, because by now it would be too fragile. A fossil tooth is not strong anymore, and it's too brittle to punch through a bone. And a fossil pelvis is too brittle to use in a test, too. Greg needed fresh bone and some kind of tooth. He needed a Big Idea.

The idea came in the shape of cast aluminum teeth and a fresh cow pelvis. He fixed the tooth onto a special machine that can measure pressure, and punched the aluminum tooth into the cow pelvis.

A *T. rex* chewed up this *Triceratops* horn, leaving this tooth mark. (Peter Larson)

< 155 >

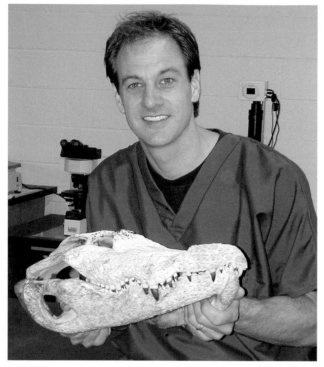

Greg Erickson studies teeth and bite marks. (Courtesy of Greg Erickson)

ones, their leg bones withstand a lot of pressure from weight and movement, causing the bone to actually rebuild itself. This erases any rings that might have been there.

So what's Greg's Big Idea about this? He's looking at everything in a new way. Instead of only looking at dinosaur leg bones, he's checking other bones in the body that carry less weight. And he's using only wild alligators (not ones in zoos, where their food and environment are regulated), so their rings will most closely resemble a *T. rex*'s lifestyle. And, to top it off, he's feeding the alligators special stuff that leaves its own rings. After several years, he can trace his experiments right in the bone.

Greg isn't saying he knows the answer yet, but maybe after some more tests, he'll be able to tell us how long it took a *T. rex* to grow.

The Molecule Detective

Ever since *Jurassic Park*, everybody has been wondering whether it's possible to clone dinosaurs. That's because in the movie, scientists grew dinosaurs in test tubes by making changes to tiny bits of dinosaur DNA taken from fossils.

In real life, in every cell, every creature carries the microscopic molecule called DNA. DNA is the command center for making more cells—more us, more grasshoppers, more elephants. It does this by telling each cell to make more cells like it—more blood, more bones, more skin. In real life, sometimes scientists can use the DNA from one creature to make a clone of the creature. This made other scientists wonder, "Hey, if we find some bits of dinosaur DNA, can we bring dinosaurs *back to life?*"

The trouble with DNA is that it isn't very

The machine's gauge said that it took 3,000 pounds per square inch to poke a hole—and it might take more to bite through a leg bone. This is even more pressure than the bite made by a lion or croc! Greg would know, because he also studies living crocodiles. He really used his head to discover that Stan could out-bite today's champion biters. What else might studies like this tell us?

In other news, Greg has been trying to solve an old bone problem. Remember how scientists have noticed that some dinosaur bones have growth rings—like a tree, where each ring represents one year's growth? They tried to compare these with alligator and bird bone growth rings, but the problem was that it's hard to say exactly what a ring represents in an animal. A growth spurt? A season? A year? A three-year drought? Plus, with dinosaurs, especially big

< 156 >

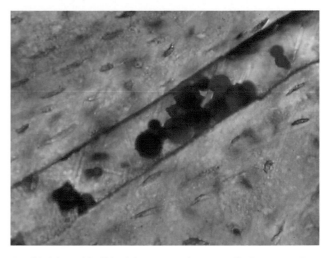

Could this red ball inside a *T. rex* bone really be part of an ancient blood cell? (Courtesy of Mary Schweitzer)

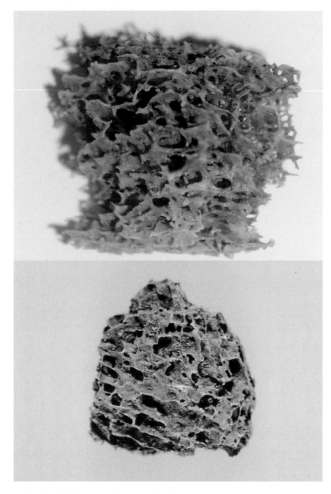

Which of these bone chunks—shown under a microscope—belongs to *T. rex,* and which to a horse that died ten year ago? (Courtesy of Mary Schweitzer)

likely to tell us anything after millions and millions of years. Water and light and microbes and other parts of nature act to break it into chunks that are too tiny for us to analyze with current scientific methods. But wait! DNA tells the cells of animals how to make proteins, and proteins are where all the interesting stuff really is. Meat and bones and hair and skin and eyes— even the *color* of your eyes!—are all the result of many proteins acting together. Since DNA makes proteins, we can find out almost as much about an animal from a good protein as we can from DNA.

Mary Schweitzer, at North Carolina State University, knew that some proteins are tightly hooked up with minerals, which makes them stable—maybe even over millions of years. She thought that if she looked at the right types of fossils for the right kinds of proteins, she might be able to find small pieces. So she started looking deep, deep inside huge *T. rex* leg bones. What did she see? First, she noticed that the inside part of the bones didn't look a whole lot different from the same parts of an old horse that had been dead only ten years.

And when Mary looked closer at the dinosaur bone, with a microscope, she saw something even more interesting: tiny channels where blood vessels once ran through the bone. And inside the channels?

Weird, tiny red "balls." She wondered, "Could these be ancient, dried out mineral leftovers of real dinosaur *blood cells*? And if they *were* blood cells, could they still have some tiny bits of the blood proteins inside? And if they *did* have proteins, could the proteins tell us anything about the dinosaurs?"

After lots and lots and lots of experiments on

< 157 >

lots and lots of different fossils—from all over the world, and from all different ages—Mary made a conclusion. It's the type of conclusion that very careful scientists make when they want to be very clear and specific:

In some cases, under very special circumstances, every now and then, dinosaur or bird bones might have some bits of original molecules that were produced by those very animals when they were alive.

So does that mean Mary or some other scientist can build a dinosaur from scratch? From "some bits of original molecules"? I don't think so. We haven't even figured out all the details of *human* DNA parts, and we have plenty of samples of that. Chances are we'll never have the tools to collect enough bits to build the whole puzzle and then incubate anybody's ancient scary eggs. I can't decide if this is a good thing (live dinosaurs would be SCARY!) or a bad thing (I'D LOVE TO SEE THEM!).

The Wing Spring

At Harvard University, Farish Jenkins wondered how to identify the purpose of certain bones in animals. He had a Big Idea of combining two old machines for a new purpose.

Wind tunnels are enclosures where the speed of wind can be controlled. Scientists can study how race cars work in the wind, or how weather patterns develop. Farish combined the wind tunnel and a moving X-ray machine, called a fluoroscope, to learn about bird skeletons. Not lying-down-dead skeletons, but living, moving skeletons!

He put a live bird in a wind tunnel, and asked it nicely to fly against the wind currents while he X-rayed its body. In this way, Farish learned

something that no one had ever even guessed! The bird's wishbone worked like a spring, helping the wing muscles do their very hard flapping job. The wishbone helped recycle the wing's energy so that the muscles didn't have to start from scratch with each flap.

How do you think a theropod dinosaur's wishbone worked?

Computer Geeks

One big advantage today's paleontologists have over the ones in the past is that we can use computers to help us test some of our Big Ideas and see if they really make sense. Here are the stories of three people who did just that. Lots of people have been arguing about how fast an extinct creature walked, or whether it could run. A paleontologist from Brown University, Steve Gatesy, was wondering the same thing. He knew that evolution had changed the position of leg bones once they went from theropods to birds—because living birds do not have a tail that balances their front ends. With the short tail, a bird's *center of gravity*, the point where the body balances, is more forward than a theropod's. This caused their upper leg bones, the femurs, to become more parallel with the ground. This means that only the lower parts of their legs

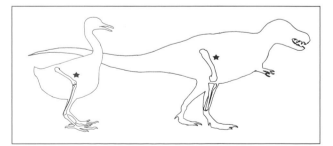

A bird's center of gravity shifted into a different place from that of its long-tailed dinosaur ancestors. (Peter Larson)

< 158 >

Steve studies how dinosaurs walked. (Courtesy of Steve Gatesy)

move as they walk. But dinosaurs' upper leg bones were more vertical than a bird's. So there's no exact living model to use.

Steve had a Big Idea to combine lots of other ideas. He uses dinosaur trackways and actual bones to create computer models. Soon he may have working models that give us our best idea yet as to how The Great Food Chase went down.

Kent Stevens, from the University of Oregon, is interested in how the long necks of sauropods worked. He wrote a whole new computer program, called Dinomorph, to make models of each bone, and then string them all together. The computer lets him move whole dinosaur skeletons around to see whether these creatures really went up, up, up, or just up. So far, the idea of reaching high up in trees to strip leaves isn't working on the computer model. What might be the problem? We just found out that Kent will be using Dinomorph on theropods, too— and soon he'll be morphing Stan. We'll keep you posted on what he finds out.

Finally, we have the story of Nathan Myhrvold, who is a non-paleontologist computer geek. He was one of the founders of Microsoft, and he has

Kent Stevens, inventor of Dinomorph. (Courtesy of Kent Stevens)

no training in biology or paleontology. But he loves fossils. And he loves computers.

Nathan wondered about the long whiplike tail of the *Diplodocus*. He used a computer to model the tail's movement. His model suggests that the ends of those thirty-foot tails could have whipped at more than 740 miles per hour—more than the speed of sound! If this was true, maybe *Diplodocus* cracked that tail like Bucky Derflinger cracks a bullwhip—except the dinosaur would have used it for self-defense. And maybe this is why we don't find the tips of many *Diplodocus* tails. Did they *snap off*?

< 159 >

Phil Currie knows more about theropods than anyone. (Clive Coy)

The Hunters

Hunting dinosaurs is not just about looking for them. It's also about having Big Ideas about what we *have or haven't* found yet. We know specialists who are experts in their own backyards or formations—like the Sacrisons or Bucky. They're looking around the Hell Creek Formation, and since they know so much about the bones there, they'll know right away if they find something brand new.

It's hard enough keeping track of your own deposit. Some people are experts at *lots* of deposits. Phil Currie, from the Royal Tyrrell Museum in Ontario, hunts for fossils all over the world. He has found new species and collected fossils from Asia, South America, and North America. He's found countless types of duckbills, *T. rex* relatives, *Triceratops* relatives, oviraptors, and *Troodons*. He may have found more species of dinosaurs on more continents than any living person. He's also the world's expert on meat-eating dinosaurs.

Phil was the first Western paleontologist to know about *Sinosauropteryx*, the Chinese theropod with downy feathers. He used to carry its picture around in his shirt pocket so he could show his paleo pals. In South America, Phil found a bunch of specimens of a brand new species related to *Giganotosaurus*, which may turn out to be the biggest theropod of all. Lots of measurements have to happen, and nearly complete specimens have to be found, to be sure. Right now, *Giganotosaurus* is in a size race against *T. rex*, *Carcharodontosaurus*, and *Acrocanthosaurus*.

< 160 >

Sometimes it pays to listen to that little voice in your head that says, "Look here!" (Ed Gerken)

Paul Sereno, of the University of Chicago, works at classifying dinosaurs and is really good at identifying what bones come from what dinosaurs. He, too, roams the globe looking at dinosaur bones—including unidentified bones found by other researchers—and he works as a *National Geographic* Explorer-in-Residence. Lately, he looked at some bones stored in a museum in India. He identified and named the new *Rajasaurus*, a large theropod with a horn on its head.

Paul's Big Idea about *Rajasaurus*: it will be able to help generalists piece together the story of how dinosaurs—and continents—were distributed across the earth so long ago. It has a relative in Madagascar.

If you choose to be a generalist, and if field work is your favorite part of paleontology, you may have some Big Ideas of where to look next. Try India, where the fossil record is sparse, or Japan—where a new *Spinosaurus* has been identified just from teeth! Or you could join Hans Larson in the arctic of Canada. He's a fun thinker, who used to work with Paul Sereno in Africa. From hot to cold places, Hans is looking in new places for new dinosaurs.

Secret tip: Knowing where to look for fossils doesn't stop with knowing how the ancient continents were positioned, and where the different piles of sediment were deposited, and where other fossils have been found. Some of the best fossil hunters also use their *instincts*. Fossil exploration, whether on the map or in the field, begins in your heart. You just get a feeling.

< 161 >

If you'd rather not *dig* as much as *think*, you could help put together the information that Phil, Paul, and their colleagues across the world have already collected. Or, you could dive into the *tons* of field jackets—some from the 1800s—that have never been opened! Every major museum has a collections department, and in paleontology, it often includes fossils that no one has had time to work on. Some institutions have hundreds of these untouched field jackets, time capsules collected decades and decades ago. What surprises do you think they might hold?

More Questions That Need Big Ideas, Hypotheses, or Even Answers
(In no particular order. Pick some you like best. MAKE UP OTHERS!)

1. How could we find fossils with remote sensing? Is there a machine we could use to look underground to see where fossils are? Is this impossible?

Ground Probing Radar may someday help us to locate dinosaur skeletons—before their bones have emerged from the ground. (Ed Gerken)

2. What about "gradual extinction" before the "real extinction"? Some paleontologists have been looking at the fossil record, saying there was a drop-off of species *before* the Cosmic Cannonball struck Earth. But other scientists are saying that isn't true. Plus, in the Hell Creek Formation, we've been finding more and more specimens. And sea creatures were plentiful, too. Were dinosaurs dying out before the Cannonball? Or not?

3. Dinosaur diseases! What were they? How did they compare to today's?

4. Hurry! Someone invent better and faster ways to clean dinosaur bones!

5. Someone else invent better ways to fill "spongy," weak bone to make it stronger during preparation!

6. What about better cameras to take photos from the air to prospect for fossils?

7. Wanted: several thousand new species.

< 162 >

8. Maybe now that animal definitions are so mixed up, we need a whole new classification system. Do "dinosaurs" really exist anymore? Do "birds"?

Many dinosaurs fall into the Ornithischian category. Pick your favorites. (Dorothy Sigler Norton)

9. Ornithischian questions:

   a) What, if anything, is an ornithischian—a classification that means "bird-hipped" but doesn't include birds? It includes *Triceratops*, duckbills, *Stegosaurus*, and *Pachycephalosaurus*.

   b) Are ornithischians really related to theropods, long-necks, and birds?

   c) How did their arms work? Not just the *Triceratops* Two-Step, but how did they attach to the chest? Everybody's arguing about this.

   d) Why do some dinos have gizzard stones and some not? Did the ones without swallow their teeth instead of rocks, to help grind up food in their stomachs? What other reasons could there be?

   e) How do we tell boys from girls in ornithischians?

10. Sauropod questions:

    a) While we're at it, how do we tell gender in sauropods?

    b) Did they have wishbones?

    c) Did they all have gizzard stones?

    d) Did they eat only plants? We have a *Camarasaurus* with pieces of *turtle* between its teeth! We still believe it ate plants, but what was that turtle doing in there? Sometimes silly questions lead somewhere exciting!

    e) How much did they really weigh? Don't forget about those weight-reducing air sacs!

    f) Would their heads really pop off if they lowered them too fast? Did they have something special in their bodies we haven't found that solves the blood-pressure problem?

    g) How tiny of a brain can you live with? What's the smallest brain necessary to operate a big, huge dinosaur?

11. Are scientists correct in counting pterosaurs as a group all to themselves? Or could they be theropods, too?

12. Invent new tools!

< 163 >

Sometimes even skin impressions are preserved. This one is from a *Triceratops*. We found at least four different textures of skin on this animal. From what part of the animal do you think this crocodile-like skin came from? (Ray Colby)

13. Will we ever know more about dinosaur skin? Try to get the last word on color, scales, and feathers.

14. How did dinosaurs grow? We need lots more specimens of eggs, embryos, babies, and kids.

15. We've found two varieties of skulls in *T. rex*. Have we made a mistake? Is *T. rex* really more than one species? Could two huge theropods have lived in the same place at the same time?

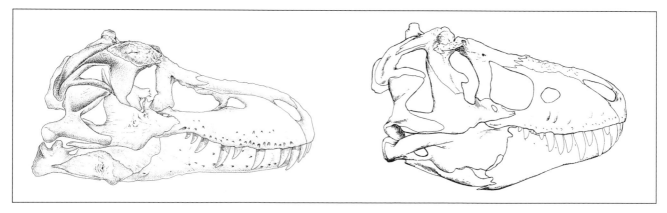

Sue's nose, *(left)* is longer and narrower than that of AMNH-5027 *(right)*. This and other characteristics *might* mean they're two different, related, dinosaurs—instead of both being *T. rex*. (*Left:* Dorothy Sigler Norton; *Right:* Peter Larson after H.F. Osborn)

< 164 >

Cool Tool: Rapid Prototype Machine

This is a pretty new machine. Maybe it will inspire you to invent another one. First you start with a CAT scanner. You remember, the one that X-rays something in slices and then puts the slices together to make a 3-D computer image of the thing. The Rapid Prototype Machine uses a CAT scanner with a tub of liquid plastic and a laser beam. I know, it sounds totally goofy, but it creates a 3-D *physical model* of whatever you're scanning.

This is how it works. There's a weird *thing* inside this one *Gorgosaurus* brain case. It's a mass of some sort that's stuck to the side of the brain case. It looks like a sponge where open spaces are filled with matrix. It could be preserved brain tissue. Or it might be a brain tumor whose blood vessels got clogged or hardened with calcium. The matrix inside the "sponge" is really hard. To get the thing off the brain case, you'd have to chip it off—and its natural form would be ruined. The part where it touches the brain case would be just a giant scrape mark. We'd like to look at the whole mass without disturbing the fossil—and without its matrix "filler."

My friend Art Anderson recommended the Rapid Prototype Machine, which takes the CAT image of the whole brain case *and* the mass. Then the computer can remove the brain case and the matrix from the image. This means that on screen you can see a computer model of *only the mass* that was inside the brain case.

Next, the machine reads those X-ray slices of the mass and directs the laser beam gadget

This is a photo of the *Gorgosaurus*'s "brain tumor" (the lighter colored mass) still in its brain case. (Ed Gerken)

to duplicate the slices within the tub of liquid plastic. Each slice is then copied in plastic, matching exactly the image on the screen. When it's done, the slices have all been hardened into one piece, and the plastic is in the exact shape of the mass. We can hold in our hands the brain tumor, or brain tissue, or whatever it turns out to be. The plastic cast will include even the empty holes where the matrix used to be.

< 165 >

Getting Started

Every good paleontologist has to start somewhere, and you know that somewhere is the library. It's also in talking with experts and mentors, in taking classes, in joining clubs, and in going out in the field. I'd like to give you some hints of where to begin searching for paleo information and experience. These are just a few ideas—use them to create your own!

The Best Books to Start With

You can find these and other titles in the library or sometimes through used booksellers. Many online book sources might have them, so you can start your own library at home.

An Introduction to the Invertebrates
Janet Moore. Cambridge, England: Cambridge University Press, 2001.

Basic Paleontology
Michael Benton and David Harper. Essex, England: Addison Wesley Longman, 1997.

The Book of Life
Stephen Jay Gould, ed. New York: W.W. Norton & Company, 2001.

The Complete Dinosaur
James O. Farlow and M.K. Brett-Surmon, ed. Bloomington, IN: Indiana University Press, 1997.

Dinosaur Digs
Blake Edgar, ed. Verlag KG, Singapore: Discovery Communications, Inc., and Apa Publishers, GmbH & Co., 1999.

(Ed Gerken)

(Larry Shaffer)

< 166 >

The Dinosaur Heresies: New Theories Unlocking the Mystery of the Dinosaurs and Their Extinction
Robert T. Bakker, Ph.D. New York: Zebra Books, Kensington Publishing Corporation, 1986.

Dinosaur Safari Guide: Tracking North America's Past
Vincenzo Costa. Stillwater, MN: Voyager Press, 1994.

The Dinosauria
David B. Weishampel, et al., eds. Berkeley, CA: University of California Press, 1990.

Dinosaurs: The Encyclopedia (with supplements)
Donald F. Glut. Jefferson, NC: McFarland & Company, Inc., 1997. Supplement 1, 2000. Supplement 2, 2002. Supplement 3, 2003.

Discovering Fossils: How to Find and Identify Remains of the Prehistoric Past
Frank A. Garcia. Mechanicsburg, PA: Stackpole Books, 2003.

Hunting Dinosaurs
Louie Psihoyos with John Knoebber. New York: Random House, 1994.

The Nature Companions: Rocks, Fossils, and Dinosaurs
Various authors. San Francisco, CA: Fog City Press, 2002.

Roadside Geology Series (more than twenty different books for different states).
Missoula, MT: Mountain Press Publishing Company.

Rex Appeal: the Amazing Story of Sue, the Dinosaur That Changed Science, the Law, and My Life
Peter Larson and Kristin Donnan. Montpelier, VT: Invisible Cities Press, 2002.

(The Toad)

Clubs and Organizations

Clubs and organizations keep you in the loop. When new finds are announced, or fun events are being planned, you'll know right away. You can keep track of what's new through their many websites—and you can attend annual lectures, field trips, and fossil shows. You already know about local rock clubs. Look up the *American Federation of Mineralogical Societies* at **www.amfed.org**, and look for the club nearest you.

You can also join the Paleo Society right away. It's an international group focusing on paleontology, and it publishes both the *Journal of Paleontology* and *Paleobiology*, along with a member newsletter called Priscum. Check them out at **www.paleosoc.org**.

There are other paleontological societies that, like the Paleo Society, are very active, publish newsletters, sponsor outings, and even conduct annual expos. Check online under "paleontological societies," but also focus in on these two. MAPS—Mid-America Paleontology Society—at **http://midamericapaleo.tripod.com**.

< 167 >

(Layne Kennedy)

And WIPS—Western Interior Paleontological Society—at **www.wipsppc.com.**

When you turn eighteen, think about a membership in the Society of Vertebrate Paleontology. This is a scientific and educational group that publishes *The Journal of Vertebrate Paleontology.* You'll find them at **www.vertpaleo.org.** Their annual meeting includes some of the newest scientific information available. It's pretty technical sometimes, but you'll be able to handle it, especially if you're planning to be a professional paleontologist!

Summer Dig Programs

More and more summer dig programs are popping up each year, which is great. This means more kids can get firsthand experience at a real excavation. I haven't been to every single dig program, and by the time you're reading this, others will have started. But let me give you a few to check out; if they don't have websites, you can write to them. I know about these, and the people who run them know what they're doing. Take time out each summer to attend a dig, so by the time you're in college you'll be better than your teacher.

Earthwatch Institute—www.earthwatch.org—is an organization that helps put the public in the field with scientific researchers. They work in many scientific areas, not just paleontology, but they have sponsored several excellent paleo adventures of various types. Check to see what's new with them.

< 168 >

(Terry Wentz)

The Mammoth Site—**www.mammothsite.com** — is a great *in situ* facility built over a deposit of many mammoths. Located in Hot Springs, South Dakota, it's very civilized, and motels are close to the site.

Old Trail Museum and Paleontology Field School—**www.oldtrailmuseum.org**— focuses on Cretaceous dinosaurs. It's headquartered in Choteau, Montana.

Paleo Park—**www.paleopark.com**—has Cretaceous digs near Hulett, Wyoming. Paleo Park includes lodging facilities and a wonderful atmosphere—and it welcomes many visitors each summer who stay for one day or many.

The Paleontological Education Preserve specializes in early ice age digs in Florida and Oligocene digs in Nebraska. They offer school field trips, member dig trips, and presentations at all times of the year. No website for this one, but you can reach Frank Garcia or Ron Shrader at PO Box 1075, Ruskin, FL 33570.

Ulrich's Fossil Quarry is near Kemmerer, Wyoming, the site for abundant Eocene fossil fishes. No website, but contact Carl Ulrich, Fossil Station #308, Kemmerer, WY 83101.

Warfield Fossil Quarry also specializes in Eocene fossil fishes found near Kemmerer, Wyoming. A campground is available on site. No website, but contact Rick Hebdon at 2072 Muddy String Road, HCR 61 Box 301, Thayne, WY 82127.

Wyoming Dinosaur Center, www.wyodino.org, is in Thermopolis, Wyoming. The dinosaurs they're digging are Jurassic Age. This is a comfortable, casual environment that can accommodate many visitors each year for one or more days at a time. Motels are located close to the site.

Finally, here's my company's place: **Black Hills Institute of Geological Research**—**www. bhigr.com**—is headquartered in Hill City, South Dakota, but we dig on ranches in exposures of various ages, including Jurassic, Cretaceous, and Oligocene. Since we provide individual attention to serious learners, we can accommodate only a small number of kids (each with an adult)—and our camping is primitive.

< 169 >

(Terry Wentz)

What to Study in School to Get a Head Start

The most important subjects a paleontologist needs to know about are geology and biology. You need geology to understand rocks, and biology to understand what fossil creatures were like when they were alive. You might find great geology information in your earth science class, and then in college you will find many different types of geology classes. Biology is essential for understanding how living creatures work. Keep in mind not only the study of animals, but also plants and even microbes.

Math is important for a jillion reasons, from measuring to sorting your data. You will use geometry for figuring how to cut into the hillside and calculating how much your *T. rex* bone block can weigh before it will squash your truck.

Physics, which helps us understand our physical world, will come in handy for levering the block down the hill, and working with the moving joints of animals. Remember the Case of the *Triceratops* Two-Step? Physics is key in helping us unlock this ongoing mystery.

Knowing chemistry will save you when mixing the preservatives to put on the bones you have found, or in reading your electron microprobe's patterns, or in understanding the chemicals in animals' bodies. Chemistry also shows us how food is digested and what to look for in fossil poop.

Art is important for many things. From

< 170 >

(The Toad)

drawing maps, to sketching fossils in the ground, to imagining what creatures looked like alive, to repairing fossils. Take drawing, painting, and sculpture.

And, of course, languages. English—or whatever language you use—will come in handy when it comes time for you to write about your own discoveries. But, since paleontologists live all over the globe—and you might go all over the globe hunting for bones—you might choose one or two languages from countries that have your favorite dinosaurs. After all, what if you thought your trusted desert guide was asking, "Where's the zamboni?"—when really he just noticed a brand new specimen of *Giganotosaurus*? Last but not least, Greek and Latin are good for your

brain, and helpful in understanding scientific names. I know most schools don't teach them anymore, but maybe you can find them anyway.

Elementary and Middle School
- Earth Science
- Geography (social studies)
- Science (anything you can get)
- Math
- Computer Science
- Art
- English
- Read all the dinosaur books you can find!

High School
- Earth Science/Geology
- Biology
- Chemistry
- Physics
- Math—Algebra, Geometry, Trigonometry, Calculus
- Computer Science
- Art
- English
- Foreign Languages!

College
- Geology—Physical Geology, Structural Geology, Glacial Geology, Historical Geology, Stratigraphy (studying the strata in the earth, the sequencing of depositions)
- Paleontology—Invertebrate (no backbones) and Vertebrate (with backbones)
- Biology—Anatomy, Comparative Anatomy (comparing relationships between different animals), Zoology, Botany, Histology (thin sections of living tissue), Pathology (diseases and injuries), Physiology

(Ed Gerken)

- Chemistry—Organic Chemistry, Physical Chemistry
- Physics
- Math—Calculus, Statistics
- Astronomy
- Computer Programming
- Art—Sculpture, Painting, Drawing
- English, and other languages, plus I dare you to find Greek and Latin

Awesome College Programs

Most universities do not offer an actual degree in paleontology, but you can specialize in paleontology within a geology or biology degree. These schools listed below not only might be your *future* college, but also *right now* might offer

courses kids can take while they're still in high school! Ask your mentor, your teacher, or a local paleontologist for help in finding out how soon you can sit through a class or attend a lecture series.

Brigham Young University, Provo, Utah

Colorado School of Mines, Golden

Columbia University, New York

Fort Hays State University, Fort Hays, Kansas

Harvard University, Cambridge, Massachusetts

Montana State University, Bozeman

North Carolina State University, Raleigh

Northern Arizona University, Flagstaff

Pennsylvania State University, University Park

< 172 >

South Dakota School of Mines and Technology, Rapid City

State University of New York, Stony Brook

University of Alaska, Fairbanks

University of Alberta, Edmonton

University of Calgary, Alberta

University of California, Berkeley

University of Chicago, Illinois

University of Colorado, Boulder

University of Florida, Gainesville

University of Kansas, Lawrence

University of Maryland, College Park

University of Michigan, Ann Arbor

University of New Orleans, Louisiana

University of Oklahoma, Norman

University of Pennsylvania, Philadelphia

University of Texas, Austin

University of Wisconsin, Madison

University of Wyoming, Laramie

Yale University, New Haven, Connecticut

Kyle. (Robert Lindsey)

You Can Do This!

Now I hope you believe that kids can make a difference in paleontology. All the kids we wrote about were making excellent finds—while learning in school *and* studying on their own. One kid we know, Kyle Lindsey, even has his own website where he hopes people will come to learn facts about his favorite fossils. Kyle fell in love with paleontology when he was four—the year *Jurassic Park* came out. Since

then, he's visited every museum he could catch a ride to, and has talked his supportive family into vacations that included everything from the American Museum of Natural History in New York to the Chicago Field Museum—where he wanted to meet Sue in person. Last summer, Kyle and his dad even came on one of our digs, where they got their hands dirty on a *Camarasaurus*.

Kyle has agreed to be our *Bones Rock* webmaster—and you can chat with him, ask questions, or make comments for our future book editions. Check Appendix E for website information.

You can create your own projects too. Think about how to use fossils for school assignments.

< 173 >

(Layne Kennedy)

Ask Social Studies or History teachers if you can do a project on how great fossil discoveries changed science through time, or caused a lot of conversation about the relationship between science and religion. Ask Science teachers if documenting the stages of preparing a fossil or investigating a paleontological problem can count as a science project. Ask Chemistry teachers about working with acid mixtures to remove difficult matrix from especially soft bone.

Teachers *love* it when kids have their own interests. You'll *love* it when you get to do what you enjoy—and get credit for it! Your parents will *love* to see you peering through a micro-

scope instead of watching TV or playing Gameboy.

Once you've fallen in love with rocks, minerals, and fossils, you have a hobby for life. You might even have a permanent job. One of the best brains in mineralogy—and another of my mentors—was Bill Roberts. He started picking up rocks at age five, and by the time he was a grown-up, he had collected rocks in seventeen countries! He had been to most of the best-known mineral localities in America—and he discovered, named, and described dozens of new minerals in South Dakota alone. Bill eventually wrote the *Encyclopedia of Minerals*, one of the most complete books on rocks ever. Maybe you

< 174 >

(Layne Kennedy)

(Layne Kennedy)

< 175 >

(Layne Kennedy)

can make these kinds of contributions to science. But if you want to be like Bill, you'll have to wear a bow tie. He always did.

Bill is an example of how one single person can make a huge impact on the world. There's another way to look at this, especially when you combine the impacts of several people. For example, more than thirty *significant* specimens of *T. rex* have been discovered. "Significant" means that the fossil is complete enough or special enough to add to what we know about its species. Not just one tail vertebra or just one rib. Of these thirty-something specimens, *only one was found by a scientist!* All the rest were found by amateur fossil hunters who just love looking for dinosaurs.

It's about being in the right place at the right time.

Did you know that a kid found the greatest archaeological discovery of the twentieth century? The Dead Sea Scrolls were a thousand years older than any other text of the Bible, and they were written a hundred years before the birth of Jesus. They were the most important manuscript discovery ever, and helped reveal the evolution of religions like Judaism, Islam, and Christianity.

This most fabulous discovery was made because Juma and his two cousins were in the right place at the right time in 1947. As usual, they were herding goats in Palestine's Judean Desert. One of Juma's goats was climbing too high on a cliff, and Juma scampered up to chase it away from danger. In the process, he threw a rock that fell inside a cave—and it clinked on something. The "clink" was a jar holding a rolled leather scroll. After archaeological crews finished their work over the next many years, they had saved about 850 artifacts, written by at least 500 different people, scattered through eleven caves. The texts were written in Hebrew, Aramaic, Greek, and Latin.

In another part of the world, fifteen-year-old Erasmus Jacobs loved playing a game with his friends. It was 1867 in Kimberly, South Africa, and the boys used small rocks as game pieces. One day Erasmus spotted a sparkly rock on his father's farm that would be perfect. He didn't realize he was playing with a diamond. Keep in mind that a nice engagement ring stone is about one *carat*—one-fifth of a gram. A standard paperclip weighs one-half gram—you would need two and a half wonderful diamonds to equal the weight of one paperclip.

Erasmus's stone weighed 10.7 carats, or 2.14 grams! About eleven engagement ring stones, four paperclips, or one dime. It also turned out to be the first diamond of what would become the greatest diamond mine in the world, called the Kimberly Mine. It produced more diamonds for a longer time than any other mine anywhere.

And guess what? A kid found the very first known evidence of *any dinosaur*. Pliny Moody was plowing a field on his father's farm in South Hadley, Massachusetts in 1802 when it happened. Pliny instantly noticed when a slab of red sandstone turned over, covered with foot-long prints that were "three-toed like a bird's." He didn't know it then, but his was the first recognized dinosaur discovery.

The first evidence of dinosaurs was found by a kid! (From Hitchcock, 1858, Ichnology of New England)

Erasmus, Juma, and Pliny changed history. Look what they did just by *being out in the world* and noticing what was around them. They were in the right place at the right time—kind of by accident. Imagine what *you* will do when you *put yourself* in the right place, at the right time, *on purpose*.

You can change history, too.

Come on, let's go.

CODE WORDS

Center of gravity	Sequoia
DNA	Significant
Fluoroscope	Speed of sound
Ornithischian	Spongy
Rapid Prototype Machine	

< 177 >

(Layne Kennedy)

< 178 >

Acknowledgments

Kid Editors

Nobody should write a book for kids without some kids to boss them around. This book was read by kids who told us where it made sense and where it didn't. They even told us where we needed more "oomph."

Katherine Bernstein, Austin Kennedy, Conor Mitchell, and Sebastian Walton, we are forever your worshipful slaves.

Left to right: Katherine Bernstein, 9, from Belmont, Massachusetts; Austin Kennedy, 13, from Minneapolis, Minnesota; Conor Mitchell, 11, from Middleton, Rhode Island; Sebastian Walton, 8, from Mt. Airy, Maryland.

Kid Webmaster

In the category of future help, thanks to Kyle Lindsey for agreeing to be our *Bones Rock!* webmaster. Who knows what *that's* going to be like. See Appendix E for information on the website.

Kid Models

Thanks to our local kids who helped in emergency photo sessions. George Bennett-Graham, Liam Counter, Dustin, Jordan, and Jill McNulty, and Adrian Munoz. (You can see Adrian and Jordan on the cover!) Thanks also to their parents for letting us shoot them.

Likewise, kids who attended our digs are depicted in these pages. Thanks for all the smiles! (Okay, okay, thanks to adults who sat still for photos too.)

< 179 >

Grown-up Editors

Nobody should write a book of any kind without Rowan Jacobsen, our pal from Invisible Cities Press. But we needed even more grown-up help, especially from Janny Banany Vogenthaler—who helped with poetry and kid-talk; Naidine Adams Larson—who kept us in perspective; Marcia Mitchell and June Zeitner—our mentors who know everything; and Kent Hups—a middle-school teacher who, along with his students, told us whether we were crazy.

Special thanks to Mary Schweitzer, who helped us nail down the details of elusive dinosaur molecules. Other great suggestions, on various topics, came from: Andrew Arntz, Bob Bakker, Julie Batsel, Larry Hutson, and even Christopher Ott—who only helped a little, but he spells dinosaur names better than Pete does.

Design

For delivery of skill above and beyond the call of friendship, lifelong gratitude to photographer Layne Kennedy and artist Dorothy Sigler Norton. Indispensable technical and photo work were gallantly provided by our knight in shining armor, Larry Shaffer. Overall book design was thoughtfully and artfully created and executed by Peter Holm.

Thanks for photo assistance to Bill Brent, and for model styling to Noelle Benjamin. Our photos of a human skull and its brain could not have been accomplished without the excellent casts provided by David Kronen of Bone Clones.

More photos provided and/or shot by Monika Adamczyk, Naidine Adams Larson, the Bernstein family, Dean E. Biggins, Black Hills Institute, Bill Brent, David Burnham, the Bury family, Ken Carpenter, Karen Chin, Ray Colby, Dan Counter, Clive Coy, Phil Currie, the Derflinger family, Edward Duke, Greg Erickson, Richard Fagan, Steve Gatesy, Ed Gerken, Jen Harvey, Rick Hebdon, Susan Hendrickson, May Hubbell, iStockphoto, Kirk Johnson, Katherine Kuhn, Mark Lane, Neal Larson, Peter Larson, the Larson family, Robert Lindsey, Dave Menke, David Mitchell, Marcia Mitchell, Don Pfritzer, Louie Psihoyos, Henry ("The Toad") Rust, Ginger Sacrison, Mary Schweitzer, Larry Shaffer, Kent Stevens, Kian Khoon Tan, Leah-Ann Thompson, U.S. Fish and Wildlife Service, the Walton family, Terry Wentz, Greg Wolkins, India Wood, Nancy Wood, June Zeitner, and Kenneth C. Zirkel.

Other illustrations provided by Bob Bakker, Ann & Michael Feinberg, Paul Janke, Lapidary Journal, Charley Parker, Pat Redman, Michael Skrepnik, and the University of Kansas.

Access

Yet another shout of appreciation to "our" landowners, who have invited us to collect in their back forties for many decades, especially the Derflinger, Munson, Niemi, and Zerbst families. Thanks also to the museums and individuals who allowed us access to their specimens, especially the American Museum of Natural History, Black Hills Institute, Black Hills Museum of Natural History, The Children's Museum of Indianapolis, The Denver Museum of Nature and Science, the Denver Zoo, and the Field Museum of Natural History.

Help!

Some people never say no to us—especially when we need dinosaur help—and for this we are eternally thankful. First, Mom and Dad Larson, who took Pete collecting. Everybody needs friends like Bob Bakker, Sara Booth, Bob Farrar, Brenda Larson, Matt Larson, Neal Larson, Larry Shaffer, and Marion Zenker. We couldn't have done it without you. Did we mention Sara Booth and Larry Shaffer? And especially Joel Bernstein, who first got our book ball rolling.

Appendix A

Scientific Names

Pronunciation and Information Guide

Name	How to say it	Age	Kind
Albertosaurus	al-BUR-ta-SORE-us	Late Cretaceous	theropod
Allosaurus	AL-o-SORE-us	Late Jurassic	theropod
Ammonite	AM-on-ite	Devonian– Late Cretaceous	extinct cephalopod
Apatosaurus	a-PAT-o-SORE-us	Late Jurassic	sauropod
Archaeopteryx	are-key-OP-trix	Late Jurassic	first bird
Bambiraptor	BAM-bee-rap-tor	Late Cretaceous	theropod
Brachiosaurus	BRACK-ee-o-SORE-us	Late Jurassic	sauropod
Brontosaurus	bron-toe-SORE-us	Late Jurassic	= Apatosaurus
Camarasaurus	ca-MARE-a-SORE-us	Late Jurassic	sauropod
Carcharodontosaurus	CAR-care-o-DON-toe-SORE-us	Late Cretaceous	theropod
Carnotaurus	CAR-no-TORE-us	Cretaceous	theropod
Caudipteryx	caw-DIP-trix (or ta-rix)	Early Cretaceous	theropod
Confuciusornis	con-FEWSH-is-OR-nus	Early Cretaceous	early bird
Deinonychus	di-NON-i-cus	Early Cretaceous	theropod
Desplatosaurus	des-PLATE-o-SORE-us	Late Cretaceous	theropod
Dimetrodon	die-MET-ro-don	Late Permian	mammal-like reptile
Edmontosaurus	ed-MONT-o-SORE-us	Latest Cretaceous	ornithischian–duckbill
Electrosaurus	ee-LEC-tro-SORE-us	Late Cretaceous	theropod
Eohippus	EE-o-HIP-us	Eocene	early horse
Equus	ECK-wuss	Holocene	horse
Fabosaurus	fab-o-SORE-us	Holocene	imaginary
Flexicalimene	flex-i-CAL-i-MEE-nee	Ordovician	trilobite– extinct arthropod
Gallimimus	gal-i-MIME-us	Late Cretaceous	theropod
Giganotosaurus	JIG-a-NO-toe-SORE-us	Late Cretaceous	theropod
Godzilla	god-ZIL-a	Holocene	imaginary
Gorgosaurus	GOR-go-SORE-us	Late Cretaceous	theropod

< 181 >

Name	How to say it	Age	Kind
Homo sapiens	HO-mo-SA-pee-ans	Late Pleistocene–Holocene	humans
Iguanodon	i-GWA-no-don	Early Cretaceous	ornithischian hadrosaur
Megalosaurus	MEG-a-lo-SORE-us	Early Cretaceous	theropod
Mesohippus	MEZ-o-HIP-us	Oligocene	horse
Microraptor	MY-crow-rap-tor	Early Cretaceous	theropod
Mononykus	ma-no-NI-kus	Late Cretaceous	theropod
Nanotyrannus	NA-no-ti-RAN-us	Latest Cretaceous	theropod
Oreodont	OR-ee-o-dont	Eocene–Miocene	sheeplike mammal
Ornithischian	OR-ni-THI-ski-an	Early Jurassic–Latest Cretaceous	plant-eating dinosaurs with short necks
Ornithomimus	OR-ni-thoe-MIME-us	Late Cretaceous	theropod
Oviraptor	OH-vi-rap-tor	Late Cretaceous	theropod
Pachycephalosaurus	pack-ee-sef-a-lo-SORE-us	Late Cretaceous	ornithischian
Parahippus	PAIR-a-HIP-us	Pliocene	horse
Paronychodon	pair-o-NICK-o-don	Late Cretaceous	theropod
Protoceratops	pro-toe-SARE-a-tops	Late Cretaceous	ornithischian horned dinosaur
Pterodactylus	tear-o-DACK-till-us	Late Jurassic	pterosaur
Pterosaur	TAIR-o-sore	Mesozoic Era	"flying reptiles"
Rajasaurus	RAH-jah-SORE-us	Late Cretaceous	theropod
Sauropod	SORE-o-pod	Early Jurassic–Latest Cretaceous	long-necked dinosaur
Sinosauropteryx	sy-no-sore-OP-trix	Early Cretaceous	theropod
Spinosaurus	SPI-no-SORE-us	Late Cretaceous	theropod
Stegosaurus	ste-go-SORE-us	Late Jurassic	ornithischian
Struthiomimus	STREW-thee-o-MIME-us	Late Cretaceous	theropod
Tarbosaurus	TAR-bow-SORE-us	Late Cretaceous	theropod
Theropod	THARE-o-pod	Late Triassic–Latest Cretaceous	meat-eating dinosaur
Triceratops	tri-SARE-a-tops	Latest Cretaceous	ornithischian horned dinosaur
Tyrannosaur	ti-RAN-o-sore	Cretaceous	theropod group
Tyrannosaurus rex (T. rex)	ti-RAN-o-SORE-us-REX TEE-rex	Latest Cretaceous	theropod
Velociraptor	ve-LA-si-rap-tor	Late Cretaceous	theropod

< 182 >

Geologic Extinction Timeline

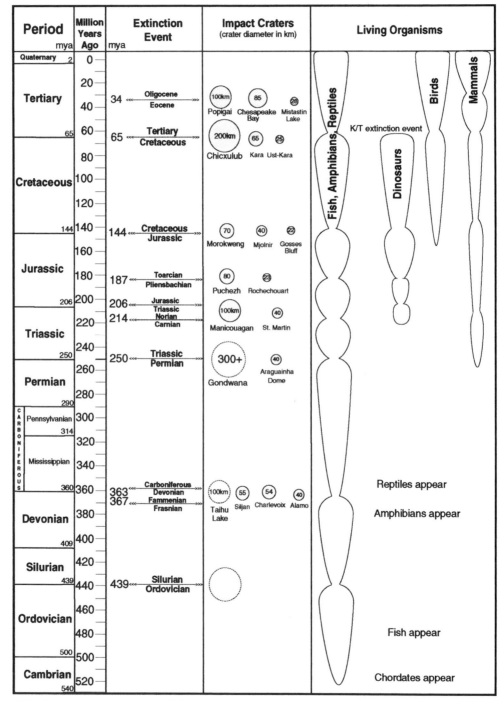

Extinctions appear to coincide with large impact events and may be one of the driving forces of evolution.

Illustration by Paul R. Janke.

< 183 >

Fossil Exploration Permission Letter Template

Date _____

My name is _____

I am in the _____ grade at my school, named:

_____ School.

I would like to explore for fossils on your property. The reason(s) for this field trip:

☐ Practice finding and/or collecting fossils
☐ A school project
☐ Personal interest
☐ Other _____

I am accompanied by at least one adult, whose name is:

_____

1. May I have permission to:
   Look for fossils here? ☐ Yes ☐ No
   Collect fossils here? ☐ Yes ☐ No
   Keep for free or buy from you any fossils I collect? ☐ Yes ☐ No

2. If I have permission would you like to come collecting with us? ☐ Yes ☐ No

3. Would you like to see what I find, or do you want a report about what I have found?
   See the fossils ☐ Yes ☐ No   Written report ☐ Yes ☐ No
   Oral report ☐ Yes ☐ No   Copy of school project (if applicable) ☐ Yes ☐ No

4. Are there any special instructions you have, such as exactly where to go, closing gates, or what to watch out for?

   _____

   _____

   _____

   _____

No matter what your answers are, thank you for your time in filling out this Permission Form!

Property Owner's name _____

Physical address _____

Mailing address _____

Telephone number _____ e-mail _____

Property Owner's signature _____

My signature _____

My mentor's signature _____

< 184 >

Appendix D

Teacher's or Independent Study Guide

Although this section is for teachers, most paleontologists are self taught. That means you shouldn't be afraid to use the Teacher's or Independent Study Guide even if you aren't a teacher! You might have fun doing these projects or answering these questions—or thinking up your own.

This book is meant to be, more or less, a general guide to becoming a paleontologist. However, it most likely accomplishes both less and more than that. That is, it is impossible in one small volume to comprehensively cover every topic involved in the study of fossils—including paleontology, geology, biology, botany, and a host of related subjects. Plus, our larger mission is to stimulate scientific curiosity—spanning topics beyond our scope.

Therefore, this book can be used as a source of information—such as learning practical steps to fossil collection and cleaning—and also as a launching point for *thinking*. In Chapter 6, for example, students are taken through a whole process of hypothesis development and testing. This theoretical process could be applied to almost any project.

You might use the Code Words at the end of each chapter for vocabulary exercises, quizzes, or to use in writing projects. Below, we have provided some sample questions and class exercises—but how about asking students to write their own multiple-choice questions as they read each chapter? Or ask students to find five of their favorite subjects in the book, and use them for research projects, class assignments, or term papers in science, history, writing, geology, English, geography, art, or any other class.

Please keep in mind that while all the questions provided below stem from the text, not all are directly answered in it! Those that are not answered specifically are meant to develop thought and research skills—and to invite the imagination of teachers and students to go wild. The subjects in this book also might lend themselves well to open-book/discovery quizzes or tests—where children interact with the material in their own way. (By the way, we don't really want to *answer* all of the included questions—that would take the fun away—but you can check our website for an answer link in a "question emergency.")

We hope you find the same thing we have noticed in countless school visits, museum presentations, and one-on-one talks with kids. Paleontology—and especially dinosaurs—tap the imagination like nothing else. I'm often asked, "What is so special about dinosaurs?" The answer has to do with fantasy, reality, and monsters. Dinosaurs once prowled the earth in the flesh. There's nothing to compare to them, as is evidenced with every dropped jaw on every

< 185 >

kid who walks up to a skeleton in a museum. (And some of those kids are older than I am!) If, through the use of this volume, you find a topic that involves the student (that may be you!), go with it. Explore it. Learn about it. And then take it in new directions. The world is just out there, waiting.

Common Sense

This book was created with the idea of listing the *best* materials for collecting, preparing, and preserving fossils. Obviously some of these may be inappropriate for younger or less responsible individuals. X-acto knives are very sharp, superglues bond everything (including skin, eyelids, even lips!), and acetone and PVA are very flammable. All of these have substitutes. Dull blades (rubbed with sandpaper), Elmer's glue, and Elmer's glue thinned with water will work just fine.

It is very important that beginning fossil collectors have mentors and that experienced fossil collectors have collecting buddies. Accidents and injuries can be compounded when one is alone—no matter how experienced one is.

Collecting buddies and class groups need permission to look for fossils on various kinds of land. Seek out private landowners or public land managers well before your trips.

Chapter 1
So, You Want to Become a Paleontologist!

How Science Works • What Exactly Is a Paleontologist Anyway? • Becoming a Fossil • The Case of the Triceratops Two-Step

Sample Questions

1. What is paleontology, and how does it differ from archaeology?

2. What is the difference between "vertebrate" and "invertebrate"?

3. What is it called when a scientist has a guess about what an answer might be to a question?

4. What is it called after the scientist tests the guess many times and thinks she has the answer?

5. What are some reasons two birds that look very similar might not be exactly alike? Does this evaluation work with other kinds of animals? If so, list three.

6. What is sediment?

7. Are all fossils fossilized? Are all fossils petrified?

8. What is one of the most important factors that ensures that an organism will become a fossil?

9. Which of the following are extinct groups? (You may choose more than one. Plus some of these are not covered in the book—use a dictionary if you need to!)
   a) Trilobites
   b) Ammonites
   c) Crocodilians
   d) Marsupials

< 186 >

e) Sauropods

f) Pterosaurs

g) Lagomorphs

h) Ornithischians

i) Crinoids

j) Arthropods

k) Echinoderms

l) Arachnids

m) Monotremes

n) Brachiopods

o) Mammals

p) Squamates

q) Cyanobacteria

r) Fungi

10. Do fossils "tell the truth" about extinct animals? Do all scientists agree with one another?

11. How do you think a *Triceratops* walked?
a) Like a lizard
b) Like a rhino
c) Unlike either of the above

12. Do you think *Velociraptor* could open doors?

Sample Projects

1. Identify Type I and Type II fossils—either from photographs or in real life.

2. Find a model of a person or an animal, hopefully one that kids can put together. How does it move? How would a scientist look at the joints to figure out how an extinct dinosaur moved?

3. Write a story about "the best dinosaur find" you can imagine. Where would you be? What kinds of rocks are there? What kind of dinosaur(s)?

Chapter 2
Collecting the Evidence

Getting Started—Where to Look • Getting Ready to Go • What It's Like to Look for Fossils and How to Do It Yourself • Digging! • Keeping Records

Sample Questions

1. Where is the best place to begin research on fossils?

2. Why do paleontologists argue?

3. What things would you consider when *looking* for a particular kind of fossil? (You may choose more than one.)
a) What color is it?
b) What environment did it live in?
c) What did it eat?
d) Where are good rock exposures?
e) How old is it?
f) Are there geologic maps for the area?
g) Were there specific hard parts that might be preserved?
h) How big was it?
i) Is it rare?
j) Who owns the land?

4. Who might help you look for fossils?

5. What is a "safe" glue that anyone can use?

6. When is it safe to go fossil collecting alone?

7. What kind of fossils might we expect to find in a microsite?

8. What are the steps used to excavate and remove a fossil from the ground?

9. Why is it important to take field notes?

< 187 >

10. What types of information might a field map provide?

11. Do you think it's ever a good idea to take part of a fossil and leave the rest behind?

12. Do you *always* need permission before entering someone's land to look for fossils?

Sample Projects

1. Invent a tool (out of common, safe materials) that scientists haven't thought of yet.

2. If you made a fabulous fossil discovery, what scientific name would you give it? What would it look like? Can you draw it? What have you learned about dinosaurs from this new discovery?

3. Have students debate with one another about a scientific theory.

4. Have students each pick a dinosaur and research how and where they would go to find it. What would they pack?

5. Make up funny "scientific" names for common items in the room, people in your family, or pals in school. Use their characters to determine how best to identify them.

Chapter 3
Sue's Clues

Sue: What We Found and How We Found It . . .
Well, Her • What It All Means • Boys or Girls • Kids

Sample Questions

1. Who is Sue?

2. Why was Sue named Sue? How do you think most dinosaurs are named?

3. Who is the champion *T. rex* tooth finder?

4. What is a "rooted" tooth, and what can it tell you about a fossil site?

5. What are pathologies, and why are they important?

6. What is exostosis?

7. How long do you think an individual dinosaur might have lived?

8. Do you think there is a way to tell boy dinosaur skeletons from girls?

9. In what kinds of animals are boys usually bigger than girls? Girls bigger than boys?

10. Why do you think young dinosaurs are rare?

11. What gave Black Beauty her name?

12. What might it mean to find adult and young dinosaurs in the same place?

Sample Projects

1. If anyone in class has broken an arm, leg, or collarbone, feel for exostosis at the injury site. Do you think the bone is stronger or weaker where it broke?

< 188 >

2. Using *skeletons only* (no obvious fleshy parts!), see if you can "map" some gracile and robust body parts in class. Perhaps outline **shoulders** on the black board—use the largest boy and the smallest girl. Or trace **arm bone** widths and shapes on paper. What about **feet**? Check elbows, hips, and head circumference.

3. Research as many examples as you can of male animals who have special "equipment" for fighting battles with other males. What about females?

Chapter 4
What to Do with Your Fossil Once You Get It Home
The Paleo Laboratory: Training to Clean Fossils • Filling in the Gaps • "Is It Real?"

Sample Questions

1. Which fossil should be your *first* preparation project?
   a) A "perfect" *T. rex* skull
   b) A nice turtle
   c) A scrappy pile of "fossil junk"
   d) A Neanderthal skull

2. Which items should not be in a beginner's preparation kit? (You may choose more than one.)
   a) An X-acto knife
   b) A CAT scanner
   c) A scribe
   d) A paint brush
   e) A laser
   f) A nuclear device

3. In **each pair** below, choose which is harder.
   a) A grinding disk or a shark's tooth
   b) A fossil bone or a finger nail
   c) Talc or a *T. rex* skull
   d) Sodium bicarbonate or dinosaur bone

4. Why should you use a dull knife to prepare fossils?

5. Why is it important to keep notes while preparing fossils?

6. What do the following tools have in common?
   a) Air scribe
   b) Pneumatic chisel
   c) Air brade
   d) Pneumatic grinder

7. What is a good tool to aid you in preparing or sorting really tiny fossils?

8. How can ultraviolet or infrared light help you in studying fossils?

9. What is the easiest way to tell a real dinosaur skeleton from a cast?

10. Why is it important to make casts of fossils?

11. Who found the first ichthyosaur and plesiosaur, and in what country?

12. What is one technique or tool that helps spot fossil fakes and also "uncovers" restoration?

Sample Projects

1. Have students collect objects that fluoresce. (Think of rocks, toys, clothes, fossils.)

< 189 >

2. Using liquid latex in multiple brushed-on coats, create molds of fossils or other objects. Once the molds have cured, plaster of paris can be poured inside to make casts. These may then be painted to resemble the original objects.

3. Save chicken bones from a family dinner. Boil them, clean them of all soft tissue, dry, and reassemble the bones. (Too bad, no head! Maybe everyone can make a new one out of, well, anything else.)

Chapter 5
Stan's Plans

The Bare Bones • Behavior

Sample Questions

1. How many bones are in a *T. rex* skull?

2. How many types of dinosaurs laid eggs?

3. What are the "characters" of a carnivore's tooth, and how do they differ from an herbivore's and an omnivore's?

4. How do crocodiles remove flesh from their unlucky "dinner dates"?

5. What do we call the "thinking part" of the brain?

6. Who has a bigger "smelling part" of the brain, a dog or a vulture?

7. Is your brain the size of:
   a) A watermelon
   b) A cleaned chicken
   c) A banana

8. Who would win a chess tournament played among the following:
   a) *T. rex*
   b) *Stegosaurus*
   c) *Diplodocus*
   d) *Velociraptor*
   e) *Triceratops*

9. Was *T. rex* a scavenger or a predator?

10. Create a story to explain the last moment in the "Dance to the Death" of the famous Mongolian *Velociraptor–Protoceratops* specimen.

11. What do you think *Triceratops* tasted like? *T. rex*?

12. If "you are what you eat," what did you have for dinner?

Sample Projects

1. Pick a dinosaur and imagine you are observing it from a treetop. Write down a series of observations about its behavior.

2. Look up illustrations of different animals' brains. Compare and contrast their parts. Who can smell well? See well? Hear well? What else can the brains tell you about these animals? Anything special?

3. Discuss whether shopping in the grocery store is a predator or a scavenger behavior.

4. Make a list of all the pets owned by students. Are they predators or scavengers? Both? What about a list of all carnivores students can think of?

5. Research the biggest egg that's ever been. How big can an egg possibly be? Why?

< 190 >

Chapter 6
Developing and Testing a Theory:
The Scientific Guessing Game

The Question • The Observations • Hypothesis #1 • Hypothesis #2 • Hypothesis #1–The Sequel • More Evidence • The Theory • Possible Conclusions

Sample Questions

1. What is the difference between a generalist and a specialist?

2. Which came first, the chicken or the egg? Why? (There is a *real answer* to this question!)

3. List five characters for a human (*Homo sapiens*).

4. What animal was the "missing link" between meat-eating dinosaurs and birds? (Hint: It was discovered in 1861.)

5. Who is credited with the "discovery" of evolution?

6. Name three characters that were once thought to be specific to birds. Is there now any bird-only character?

7. *Bambiraptor* was special because:
   a) It was a juvenile
   b) It was a close relative of *Velociraptor*
   c) It had a very large brain
   d) It had a wishbone
   e) All of the above

8. Did any birds have teeth?

9. What is special about the way birds breathe?
   a) They have a system of air sacs
   b) They have relatively small lungs
   c) They have a "one-way" respiratory system
   e) All of the above

10. What animals breathed like a bird? (You may choose more than one.)
    a) Mammals
    b) Theropods
    c) Sauropods
    d) Ornithischians
    e) Crocodiles
    f) Pterosaurs

11. What could cause a sauropod to have head problems?
    a) High blood pressure
    b) Family difficulties
    c) Being on a theropod's dinner menu
    d) Fermented fruit
    e) Miniscule brain
    f) All of the above

12. Describe a theropod nest.

Sample Projects

1. Research the difference between a comet, meteor, moon, meteorite, planet, and asteroid. How are they alike and different? Why was the one that created the Chicxulub crater an "asteroid"? Look up some other famous extraterrestrial objects.

2. Read about a famous *recent* earthquake, tsunami, or natural disaster. How did it affect the way the earth looks now? Ten thousand years from now?

3. Trace the evolution of a family of creatures. How did their bodies change? Why do you think these changes occurred?

4. Pretend for a moment that birds did not come from dinosaurs. Think of other

< 191 >

animals with similar characters from which they might have evolved.

5. What would the earth be like if the asteroid hadn't crashed and created the Chicxulub crater?

makes you think they're mistakes? What might you change about these creatures?

2. Write a sample letter (for real or just for fun) to a famous paleontologist whose work you most admire. Whom would you choose, and what would you ask?

Chapter 7
Your Future Job

Help! • More Questions That Need Big Ideas, Hypotheses, or Even Answers • Getting Started • The Best Books to Start With • Clubs and Organizations • Summer Dig Programs • What to Study in School to Get a Head Start • You Can Do This!

Sample Questions

1. What would you study as a paleontologist? Are you a specialist, a generalist, a geologist, a botanist? What are your favorite aspects of the science of paleontology? If you're interested in subjects other than paleontology, what else might you study?

2. What would you most hope to discover?

3. Who was your favorite kid paleontologist discussed in the book? Why?

4. If you were able to use any technological equipment—computers, CAT scanners, *anything*—what dinosaur problem would you like to solve?

Sample Projects

1. Watch *Jurassic Park, Dinosaur,* and various documentaries on dinosaurs. Do you think the dinosaurs are moving and behaving correctly, or in ways with which you agree? Do you see any mistakes? What

Fun Books and References

The Complete Dinosaur Dictionary
Donald F. Glut. New York: Carol Publishing Group, 1982.

The Dinosaur Heresies: New Theories Unlocking the Mystery of the Dinosaurs and Their Extinction
Robert T. Bakker, PhD. New York: Kensington Publishing Co., 1996.

The Dinosaur Scrapbook
Donald F. Glut. Secaucus, NJ: The Citadel Press, 1980.

The Dinosauria
David B. Weishampel, *et al.*, eds. Berkeley, CA: University of California Press, 1990.

Dinosaurs: The Encyclopedia (with supplements)
Donald F. Glut. Jefferson, NC: McFarland & Company, Inc., 1997. Supplement 1, 2000. Supplement 2, 2002. Supplement 3, 2003.

Encyclopedia of Dinosaurs
Philip J. Currie and Kevin Padian, eds. San Diego, CA: Academic Press, 1997.

A Guide to the Fossil Footprints of the World
Martin Lockley. Denver: Lockley & Peterson, 2002.

The Illustrated Encyclopedia of Pterosaurs
Dr. Peter Wellnhofer. London: Salamander Books Limited, 1991.

T. Rex to Go: Build Your Own from Chicken Bones
Chris McGowan. New York: HarperCollins, 1999.

< 192 >

Planning Field Trips

Museum trips are always a fun time for students. Most large museums have someone on staff to assist teachers in planning a visit and often provide tour guides. A visit by the teacher to the facility beforehand can prove very useful in planning questions and discussion topics or creating study projects. Getting to know your museum's geologists or paleontologists might also gain good opportunities for laboratory visits. Longer field trips to more distant museums are also very rewarding if at all practical.

Collecting field trips are more difficult to prepare and harder to control. In addition to library research, collecting sites may be located by visiting with local geologists, paleontologists, museum personnel, or rock clubs. These people may also be willing to help with arrangements, including gaining permissions and providing instruction. Local land management agencies (city, country, state, and federal) may also be called upon for site location and permissions. Landowners should be filled in on all the details and encouraged to be present during the outing. Kids will get dirty, and so will the bus. If your local museum has an actual dig, perhaps it will be up for a visit from your class.

Help with Answering Questions

Students often ask the most marvelous, thought provoking—and difficult—questions. Don't be afraid of questions whose answers you don't know (or the kids who ask them). When I'm faced with mystery questions (which is often), I think about ways we can explore different answers together. Some of these moments have even led to research topics! In a class setting, my advice would be to use mystery questions as a basis for group discussion and investigation—and as an illustration of the scientific process. Remember, even though many individual scientists think they know "the right answer"—or even that there *is* a right answer—debate among paleontologists shows that often you really might be searching for *valid options*. This makes it much more fun and interesting to debate the "facts" your students discover.

Begin the journey into finding answers with a library research project. Try breaking down the general subject into elements—each of which can be assigned to an individual, pair, or group of students. (The teacher can be directly involved as one of the researchers, too.)

Further research might involve contacting your nearest experts—and may lead to a field trip. Maybe you've met someone from your local museum, the library, the local rock club, or an amateur paleontologist (many amateurs are *very* knowledgeable). You can also get specialized information online from the websites of some of the larger museums. Look for an "ask our staff" area, or check for links to the subject you have in mind. Often these institutions have scientists who conduct interesting, cutting-edge research, and they may have lots of information. It may not be *exactly* what you're looking for, but a related specialty area may stimulate even more inquiry. Try:

The Academy of Natural Sciences of Philadelphia — **www.acnatsci.org**

The American Museum of Natural History — **www.amnh.org**

Black Hills Institute of Geological Research —
www.bhigr.com

The Children's Museum of Indianapolis —
www.childrensmuseum.org

The Denver Museum of Nature and Science
— www.dmns.org

The Field Museum of Natural History —
www.fmnh.org

North American Museum of Ancient Life —
www.thanksgivingpoint.com/museum

The Museum of Geology, South Dakota
School of Mines —
www.sdsmt.edu/services/museum

Museum of the Rockies —
www.museumoftherockies.org

The Natural History Museum of Los Angeles
County — www.nhm.org

Project Exploration —
www.projectexploration.org

The Royal Tyrrell Museum of Palaeontology
— www.tyrrellmuseum.com

San Diego Natural History Museum —
www.sdnhm.org

The Smithsonian Institution, National
Museum of Natural History —
www.mnh.si.edu

Appendix E

Bones Rock!
Website Information

This is Kyle. He'll be welcoming your comments, suggestions, ideas, or questions at our *Bones Rock!* link through his very own website called **rexburgonline.net**. If necessary, teachers can check there for answers to our Teacher's Guide questions . . . or whatever else we think of that you *or* your teacher might want to know. Just check Kyle's site for appropriate links to *Bones Rock!*

Who is this Kyle Lindsey fella? Now fourteen years old, Kyle became a dinosaur fan at the age of four. Since then he's visited lots of museums, been on a dinosaur dig, and hung out personally with famous paleontologists. Along with his interests in paleontology and computers, Kyle also plays the viola both at church and in the school orchestra, plays tennis on his school's team, and works on the yearbook. As if that's not enough, he's developing his artistic talents, as well as photography and graphic arts, to flesh out books he hopes to write in the future. Kyle's Big Idea is to become "one of the leading experts on Texas vertebrate and invertebrate fossils and to prove whether or not *Tyrannosaurus rex* really did live in Big Bend."

Phew. He sounds pretty busy to me. Thanks, Kyle, for making time for *Bones Rock!*

< 195 >

Glossary

Please note: This Glossary is printed in Magic Ink. We'd love for you to be able to define these words yourself, from reading the chapters, so Poof! You can't see these definitions unless you've already read the whole book and you're using the Glossary as a reference for a research paper or something.

Air sacs — The most important part of the efficient bird's breathing system, these sacs allow for a one-way path for oxygen through the lungs. Air sacs also cause hollow spaces in bones.

Amber — Fossilized tree sap.

Ammonites — Extinct relatives of the squid, whose shells make beautiful fossils.

Archaeologist, archaeology — Archaeology is the study of ancient people and what they left behind. An archaeologist is the scientist who works in archaeology.

Archaeopteryx — The creature that provided the missing link between dinosaurs and birds.

Articulated — Together, and in a natural position. In paleontology, this has to do with the bones in a fossil being in the same position they were when the animal was alive.

Asteroid — A rock in space that orbits the sun—and sometimes crashes into Earth.

Binocular vision — When an animal's eyes both face forward, they can see depth of field.

Biologist, biology — Biology is the study of living animals. A biologist is the scientist who studies biology.

Bone map — A map drawn at a paleontological site that shows the positions of all the bones before they are removed from the ground.

Botanist, botany — Botany is the study of plants. A botanist studies botany.

Brain case — The part of the skull that held an animal's brain.

Cannibal, cannibalism — A cannibal is a creature that eats its own species. Cannibalism is what this practice is called.

Carbon dioxide — The "exhaust" of the breathing system, what's left over after oxygen is breathed in and processed by the body.

Cast replica — A replica of something. In paleontology, this usually means a plastic copy of a bone or skeleton.

CAT scan — Computer Axial Tomography is a three-dimensional X-ray technique that allows scientists to "look inside" fossils without cutting them open.

Center of gravity — The balance point inside something. The center of a ball, the fulcrum of a teeter-totter, etc.

Cerebrum — The "thinking part" of the brain.

Character — A feature or part of a creature that helps distinguish it from other creatures.

Chemist, chemistry — Chemistry is the study of substances, especially at the levels of atoms and molecules. A chemist is someone who does this.

Chevron — A bone under the tail, especially important when determining the gender of a skeleton.

Chicxulub crater — A crater in the Gulf of Mexico

< 196 >

and Yucutan Peninsula where scientists think the asteroid that caused dinosaur extinction impacted Earth.

Clay — Very, very fine dirt.

Claystone — Ancient clay that has become rock, which may be soft or hard.

Clone, cloned — A clone is a replica, or copy. To be cloned is to be copied.

Cold-blooded — Also called ectothermic, a cold-blooded creature relies upon the environment to regulate its body temperature. Contrasted with warm-blooded.

Cretaceous Period — A geologic period spanning 144 to 65 million years ago. (See Appendix B for the geologic extinction timeline.)

Cutting teeth — Teeth that are sharp and able to cut through meat, and even bone.

Cyanoacrylates — The material from which super-glues are made.

DNA — Deoxyribonucleic acid, the basic genetic component of life.

Depth of field — The ability to see how far things are away from the viewer. With binocular vision, seeing in three dimensions is easy, and it helps predators to hunt.

Dinosauria — The group name given to all dinosaurs in 1842.

Disarticulated — Not in its original position. In paleontology, this means bones are pulled apart from each other.

Dorsal — Part of the back, or relating to the back of a creature.

Electron microprobe — A machine that points an X-ray beam at a piece of rock or a fossil. Each mineral in the rock or fossil creates a unique pattern that helps scientists identify it.

Engineer, engineering — Engineering is the science of the design and construction of buildings and other mechanical objects. An engineer is the scientist who does this.

Eocene Epoch — A geologic time spanning from 55 to 34 million years ago. (See Appendix B for the geologic extinction timeline.)

Ethmoid — A bone that separates sections of the smelling part of the brain.

Evolution — The change of living beings through time, particularly as they develop from one species into another.

Exhale — To breathe out.

Exostosis — Extra bone growth that can occur when a bone has been broken and is healing.

Extinction events — Periods through time when a significant percentage of life is killed off through various catastrophic environmental events.

Field jacket — A plaster covering that protects fossils as they are removed from the ground.

Fissures — Fractures in bone and rock where they naturally break apart.

Fluoresce, fluorescent — To fluoresce is when minerals glow with bright colors under ultraviolet or infrared light. Fluorescent is an adjective describing those kinds of minerals.

Fluoroscope — A moving X-ray machine. This is the one that took pictures of a bird flying in a wind tunnel.

Fossilization — The process that turns something into a fossil. This means the plant or animal is quickly covered by sediment and preserved.

Fossils — Animals or plants that die and are preserved in sediments.

Fratricide — The practice of killing one's brother.

Frill — The bony "collar" worn by some dinosaurs, like *Triceratops*.

Furcula — The scientific name for "wishbone."

Gastroliths — The same as gizzard stones, except only in dinosaurs.

Gemologist, gemology — Gemology is the study of gemstones. A gemologist is a scientist who does this.

Gender — The sex of a creature or a person. Boy or girl.

Generalist — In paleontology, a scientist who works in many different areas. Contrasted with "specialist."

Geologist, geology — Geology is the study of the earth's layers. A geologist is a scientist who does this.

Gizzard stones — Rocks swallowed by creatures (birds and dinosaurs) that don't have mashing teeth (or any teeth). In the belly, the gizzard stones mash up their food.

Global Positioning System (GPS) — A machine that uses at least three satellite signals to pinpoint where one is standing on the Earth's surface

Gracile — The more delicate of two body types, gracile and robust.

Hallux — A backward-pointing big toe that nearly all birds have. It is used for perching and grasping.

Holocene Epoch — A geologic time spanning from 10,000 years ago to the present. (See Appendix B for the geologic / extinction timeline.)

Homo sapiens — The scientific name for humans.

Hypocladium — The middle part of a bird-like wishbone, the part that sticks up in the middle.

Hypothesis, hypotheses (pl.) — An educated guess. With evidence, hypotheses become theories.

Impression — A mold, or imprint, of a fossil in sediment.

Infrared light — Light with a different wavelength than light we can see with our eyes. When infrared light is shined on minerals or fossils, the objects glow with colors that help scientists identify them.

Inhale — To breathe in.

Invertebrate — A creature without a backbone.

Jurassic Period — A geologic period spanning 206 to 144 million years ago. (See Appendix B for the geologic / extinction timeline.)

Landowner — A person or group owning property. Paleontologists must always ask landowners for permission before entering their property to look for or collect fossils.

Mashing teeth — Teeth that are good for mashing food. Often found in the mouths of vegetarians, or creatures who eat different kinds of food.

Matrix — The dirt surrounding a fossil.

Mentor — The adult or at least older person who can help a student learn about fossils—or anything else, for that matter.

Mesozoic Era — A geologic time including the Triassic (250–206 mya), Jurassic (206–144 mya), and Cretaceous (144–65 mya) Periods. (See Appendix B for the geologic extinction timeline.)

Microsite — A fossil site with a concentration of very small fossils.

Miocene Epoch — A geologic time spanning from 23 to 5 million years ago. (See Appendix B for the geologic extinction timeline.)

Mold — When sediment naturally hardens around an original plant or animal, and then bacteria dissolves the plant or animal, leaving an empty shell. Also, a scientist can fabricate a mold around a fossil, out of various materials, in order to pour a cast.

Mounting — Putting together a specimen, especially a skeleton.

"Mushrooming" — Digging the sediment from around the sides of a fossil, and then creating a "stem" under it so a paleontologist can securely wrap and protect it. When a fossil is perched on its stem this way, it resembles a mushroom.

mya — An abbreviation for "million years ago."

Observation — A fact or behavior that helps a scientist develop, prove, or disprove a hypothesis.

Oligocene Epoch — A geologic time spanning 34 to 23 million years ago. (See Appendix B for the geologic extinction timeline.)

Ontogeny — How a creature grows and changes in its lifetime.

Ornithischian — A classification of dinosaurs that means "bird-hipped" but doesn't include birds. It includes *Triceratops*, duckbills, *Stegosaurus*, and *Pachycephalosaurus*.

Overburden — The layer of sediment over the layer

< 198 >

of bones at a fossil site. Overburden can be a few inches or dozens of feet thick.

Oviduct — The tube in an egg-laying female creature where eggs are produced and through which they are laid.

Oxygen — What we breathe.

Paleontologist, paleontology — Paleontology is the study of ancient life—plants and animals usually more than 10,000 years old. Paleontologists are scientists who might study any of these, or a combination: paleontology, geology, biology, or botany.

Pathology — In a fossil, evidence of an injury the creature sustained when it was alive.

Petrified, petrification — When something turns to stone. This is different from fossilization, where actual parts of the original creature remain.

Phosphate — A chemical that animals produce, which helps scientists learn about fossil poop.

Physicist, physics — Physics is the study of how our world works—things like matter, energy, force, and motion. A physicist is someone who studies those things.

Pliocene Epoch — A geologic time spanning from five to two million years ago. (See Appendix B for the geologic extinction timeline.)

Polyvinyl acetate (PVA) — A sealant used to protect fossils.

Predator — A creature that hunts for and eats other animals. Contrasted with "scavenger."

Preparation, preparatory — Preparation is the process of cleaning and preserving fossils. A preparatory is the laboratory where preparation occurs.

Preservation — How a fossil is protected in the earth.

Primates — A group of mammals—including humans, apes, and monkeys—with some shared characters, such as large brains.

Pterosaurs — A group called "flying reptiles," even though they were warm-blooded, while reptiles aren't.

Pubis — A pelvic bone that became important in the process of deciding whether birds and dinosaurs were related.

Pygostyle — Fused tail vertebrae, in birds, that form a "rudder" for steering in flight—through air *or* water.

Rapid Prototype Machine — An extra-deluxe CAT-scan machine that uses plastic to create a three-dimensional physical model of whatever is being scanned.

Reconstruction — The process of fabricating missing parts in fossils.

Relative — In this book, relative refers to comparing one thing to another, like how big one's brain is compared to its body size.

Robust — The more heavily built of two body types, gracile and robust.

Rooted tooth — A tooth that still has its root, the part that anchors it into a jawbone. In fossils, roots are important because they mean that a tooth rotted out of the skull of the animal, instead of being broken out. Contrasted with "shed tooth."

Sand — A type of soil in which fossils may be deposited.

Sandstone — Ancient sand that has become rock, which may be loose or hard.

Sauropod — A group of dinosaurs that specifically includes long-necked species.

Scavenger — A creature that eats animals that are already dead. Scavengers are also known to kill other animals if necessary. Contrasted with "predator."

Sediment — Sand or silt deposited by water, wind, or ice—and that preserves fossils.

Sedimentary rock — The rock that is formed as millions of years' worth of sediment piles up and hardens.

Sequoia — A large, coniferous tree whose cones are found as fossils.

Serrations — The jagged edges of a tooth that help it cut.

< 199 >

Shed tooth — A tooth that has been broken from the jaw, either through eating or fighting. Contrasted with "rooted tooth."

Siblings — Brothers or sisters.

Significant — In paleontology, "significant" means a fossil is important scientifically.

Silt — Very fine soil.

Siltstone — Ancient silt that has become rock, which may be soft or hard.

Sinkhole — A hole developed from underground water flowing into cracks in the sediment of a hill. Sinkholes can pull earth, bones, and rocks up to hundreds of feet underground.

Soil — The topmost layer of the earth where plants grow.

Specialist — In paleontology, a scientist who works in one specific area. Contrasted with "generalist."

Speed of sound — How fast sound moves, 740 miles per hour.

Spongy bone — Unlike solid, good quality bone, spongy bone has lots of holes and passage ways, like a sponge. This type of bone usually formed in an infected area, where bacteria invaded the bone.

Sternum — Breast bone.

Tail drag — In a trackway, the rare mark of where an ancient creature's tail dragged in the sediment as it walked.

Theory — A preferred hypothesis, one that has been isolated and accepted based on evidence.

Theropod — A group of dinosaurs that specifically includes meat-eating species.

Trackway — Fossil footprints. A trackway can include the footprints of many different individuals or kinds of dinosaurs, or just one.

Triassic Period — A geologic period spanning 250 to 206 million years ago. (See Appendix B for the geologic extinction timeline.)

Tsunami — A tidal wave, usually caused as a result of natural events like earthquakes.

Ultraviolet light — Light with a different wavelength than light we can see with our eyes. When ultraviolet light is shined on minerals or fossils, the objects glow with colors that help scientists identify them.

Vertebrate — A creature with a backbone.

Warm-blooded — Also called endothermic, a warm-blooded creature regulates its body temperature independent of the environment, usually with hair, feathers, or fur. Contrasted with cold-blooded.

Wishbone — Collarbones that fused together through evolution. Some tests show that wishbones provide "spring" for bird wings, allowing birds to fly with less effort.

< 200 >

References

Alvarez, L., Alvarez, W., Asero, F., and Michel, H. "Extraterrestrial Cause for the Cretaceous-Tertiary Extinction, Experimental Results and Theoretical Interpretation." *Science* 208, 6 June 1980: 1095–1107.

Alvarez, W., Claeys, P., and Kieffer, S. "Emplacement of Cretaceous-Tertiary Boundary Shocked Quartz from Chicxulub Crater." *Science* 269, 18 Aug. 1996: 930–935.

Attenborough, D. *The Life of Birds.* Princeton, NJ: Princeton Univ. Press, 1998.

Bakker, R.T. *The Dinosaur Heresies: New Theories Unlocking the Mystery of the Dinosaurs and Their Extinction.* New York: Zebra Books, 1986.

_____. "Inside the Head of a Tiny *T. Rex.*" *Discover,* March 1992: 58–69.

Bellairs, A. *The Life of Reptiles,* Vol. 2. New York: Universe Books, 1970.

Benton, M. and Harper, D. *Basic Paleontology.* Essex, England: Addison Wesley Longman, 1997.

Britt, B.B. "Pneumatic Postcranial Bones in Dinosaurs and Other Archosaurs." Alberta: University of Calgary, Department of Geology and Geophysics Dissertation, 1993.

Brochu, C.A. "Osteology of *Tyrannosaurus rex*: Insights from a Nearly Complete Skeleton and High-Resolution Computed Tomographic Analysis of the Skull." *Journal of Vertebrate Paleontology* 20, Memoir 7, Supplement to Number 4, January 2003.

Brooke, M. and Birkhead, T. (eds.). *The Cambridge Encyclopedia of Ornithology.* Cambridge, England: Cambridge University Press, 1991.

Carpenter, K. "Variations in *Tyrannosaurus rex.*" in *Dinosaur Systematics,* K. Carpenter and P. Currie (eds.): 141–145. Cambridge, MA: Cambridge University Press, 1990.

_____. "Evidence of Predatory Behavior by Carnivorous Dinosaurs." in *Gaia (Aspects of Theropod Paleobiology),* B.P. Perez et al. (eds.): 135–144, Lisbon, Portugal: Museu de Historia Natural, 1998.

Carpenter, K. and Alf, K. "Global Distribution of Dinosaur Eggs, Nests and Babies." in *Dinosaur Eggs and Babies,* K. Carpenter, K.F. Hirsch, and J.R. Horner (eds.): 15–30. Cambridge, MA: Cambridge University Press, 1995.

Carpenter, K. and Smith, M. "Forelimb Osteology and Biomechanics of *Tyrannosaurus rex.*" in *Mesozoic Vertebrate Life: New Research Inspired by the Paleontology of Philip J. Currie,* D. Tanke and K. Carpenter (eds.): 90–116. Bloomington, IN: Indiana University Press, Bloomington, 2001.

Colbert, E.H. "The Triassic Dinosaur *Coelophysis.*" *Museum of Northern Arizona Bulletin* 5, 1989: 71–174.

Coombs, W.P. "Modern Analogs for Dinosaur Nesting and Parental Behavior." in *Paleobiology of the Dinosaurs,* J. Farlow (ed.). Boulder, CO: Geological Society of America Special Paper No. 238, 1989: 21–53.

_____. "Behavior Patterns of Dinosaurs." in *The Dinosauria,* D.B. Weishampel, P. Dodson, and H. Osmolska (eds.): 32–42. Berkeley, CA: University of California Press, Berkeley, 1990.

Costa, V. *Dinosaur Safari Guide: Tracking North America's Past.* Stillwater, MN: Voyager Press, 1994.

Currie, P.J. "Cranial Anatomy of *Stenonychosaurus inequalis* (Saurischia, Theropoda) and Its Bearing on the Origin of Birds." *Canadian Journal of Earth Science* 22, 1985: 1643–1658.

_____. "Black Beauty." Tokyo: Gakken Mook, *Dino Frontline* 4, 1993: 22–36.

_____. "The Great Dinosaur Egg Hunt." *National Geographic* 189 (5), 1996: 96–111.

Currie, P.J. and Padian, K, eds. *Encyclopedia of Dinosaurs.* San Diego, CA: Academic Press, 1997.

de Beer, G. Archaeopteryx lithographica: *A Study Based on the British Museum Specimen.* London: British Museum of Natural History Publication No. 224, 1954.

Dietz, R. "Demise of the Dinosaurs: Mystery Solved?" *Astronomy* 19 (97), July 1991: 30–37.

< 201 >

Dodson, P. "Quantitative Aspects of Relative Growth and Sexual Dimorphism in *Protoceratops.*" *Journal of Paleontology* 50, 1976: 929–940.

_____. *The Horned Dinosaurs.* Princeton, NJ: Princeton University Press, 1996.

Dodson, P. and Tatautrov, L. "Dinosaur Extinction." *in The Dinosauria.* D. B. Weishampel, P. Dodson, and H. Osmolska (eds.): 55–62. Berkeley, CA: University of California Press, 1990.

Eaton, G.F. "Osteology of *Pteranodon.*" New Haven, CT: *Connecticut Academy of Science Memoir* 2, 1910: 1–38.

Edgar, B., ed. *Dinosaur Digs.* Verlag KG, Singapore: Discovery Communications, Inc., and Apa Publishers, GmbH & Co., 1999.

Erickson, G.M. "Incremental Lines of von Ebner in Dinosaurs and the Assessment of Tooth Replacement Rates Using Growth Line Counts." Washington, DC: *National Academy of Science Proceedings* 93 (1996): 14623–14627.

Estes, R.D. "Fossil Vertebrates from the Late Cretaceous Lance Formation, Eastern Wyoming." *Geological Science* 49, 1964: 1–180.

_____. *The Behavioral Guide to African Mammals.* Berkeley, CA: University of California Press, 1991.

Estes, R.D. and Berberian, P. 1970. "Paleoecology of a Late Cretaceous Vertebrate Community from Montana." *Breviona* 343, 1970: 1–35.

Evans, H.E. and de Lahunta, A. *Miller's Guide to the Dissection of the Dog.* Philadelphia, PA: W.B. Saunders Company, 1988.

Farlow, J.O. and Brett-Surmon, M.K., eds. *The Complete Dinosaur.* Bloomington, IN: Indiana University Press, 1997.

Farlow, J.O., Smith, M.B., and Robinson, J.M. "Body Mass, Bone 'Strength Indicator,' and Cursorial Potential of *Tyrannosaurus rex.*" *Journal of Vertebrate Paleontology* 15 (4), 1995: 713–725.

Farrar, R. "*Tyrannosaurus rex* Walking and Running Speed." Black Hills Institute publication (1995): 1.

Garcia, F.A. *Discovering Fossils: How to Find and Identify Remains of the Prehistoric Past.* Mechanicsburg, PA: Stackpole Books, 2003.

Gill, F.B. *Ornithology,* Second Edition. New York: W.H. Freeman and Company, 1995.

Glut, D.F. *The Complete Dinosaur Dictionary.* New York: Carol Publishing Group, 1982.

_____. *The Dinosaur Scrapbook.* Secaucus, NJ: The Citadel Press, 1980.

_____. *Dinosaurs: The Encyclopedia* (with supplements). Jefferson, NC: McFarland & Company, Inc., 1997. Supplement 1, 2000. Supplement 2, 2002. Supplement 3, 2003.

Gould, S.J., ed. *The Book of Life.* New York: W.W. Norton & Company, 2001.

Harter, J. *Animals: 1419 Copyright-Free Illustrations of Mammals, Birds, Fish, Insects, etc. A Pictorial Archive from Nineteenth-Century Sources.* New York: Dover Publications, Inc., 1979.

Hirsch, K.F. and Zelenitsky, D.K. "Dinosaur Eggs: The Identification and Classification." *in Dinofest International: Proceedings of a Symposium Held at Arizona State University,* D. Wolberg, E. Stump, and G. Rosenberg (eds.): 279–286. Philadelphia: The Academy of Natural Sciences, 1997.

Hitchcock, E.B. *Ichnology of New England: A Report on the Sandstone of the Connecticut Valley, Especially Its Fossil Footmarks.* Boston: William White, 1858.

Holtz, T.R., Jr. "Phylogenetic Taxonomy of the Coelurosauria (Dinosauria: Theropoda)." *in Journal of Paleontology* 70 (3), 1996: 536–538.

Horner, J. R. "Ecological and Behavioral Implications Derived from a Dinosaur Nesting Site." *in Dinosaurs Past and Present* 2, S. Czerkas and E. Olson (eds.): 51–63. Seattle: University of Washington Press, 1987.

_____. "Steak Knives, Beady Eyes and Tiny Little Arms (A Portrait of *T. rex* as a Scavenger)." *in Dinofest: Proceedings of a Conference for the General Public,* G. Rosenberg and D. Wolberg (eds): 157–164. Knoxville, TN: Department of Geological Sciences, The University of Tennessee, 1994.

Horner, J.R. and Lessem, D. *The Complete* T. rex. New York: Touchstone, Simon and Schuster, 1993.

Johnson, K.R. "Hell Creek Flora." *In The Encyclopedia of Dinosaurs,* P. J. Currie and K. Padian (eds.): 300–302. San Diego: Academic Press, 1997.

< 202 >

Kardong, K.V. *Vertebrates: Comparative Anatomy, Function, Evolution.* New York: McGraw-Hill, 1998.

Kring, D. "The Dimensions of the Chicxulub Impact Crater and Impact Melt Sheet." *Journal of Geophysical Research* 108 (E8), 1995: 16976–16986.

Larson, P.L. "The Black Hills Institute *Tyrannosaurus rex* — A Preliminary Report." *Journal of Vertebrate Paleontology* Abstract II (3); September 1991: 41A–42A.

_____. "*Tyrannosaurus* sex." *in Dinofest: Proceedings of a Conference for the General Public,* G. Rosenberg and D. Wolberg (eds.): 139–155. Knoxville, TN: Department of Geological Sciences, The University of Tennessee, 1994.

_____. "To Sex a Rex." *in Nature Australia,* Spring 1995: 45–53.

_____. "Do Dinosaurs Have Class: The Implications of the Avian Respiratory System." *in Dinofest International: Proceedings of a Symposium Held at Arizona State University,* D. Wolberg and G. Rosenberg (eds.): 105–111. Philadelphia: The Academy of Natural Sciences, 1997.

_____. "The King's New Clothes: A Fresh Look at *Tyrannosaurus rex.*" *in Dinofest International: Proceedings of a Symposium Held at Arizona State University,* D. Wolberg and G. Rosenberg (eds.): 65–71. Philadelphia: The Academy of Natural Sciences, 1997.

Larson, P. and Donnan, K. *Rex Appeal: The Amazing Story of Sue, the Dinosaur That Changed Science, the Law, and My Life.* Montpelier, VT: Invisible Cities Press, 2002.

Larson, P.L. and Frey, E. "Sexual Dimorphism in the Abundant Upper Cretaceous Therapod, *Tyrannosaurus rex.*" *Journal of Vertebrate Paleontology* 12, Abstract 96 (Supplement to No. 3), 3 September 1992: 38a.

Lockley, M. *A Guide to the Fossil Footprints of the World.* Denver, CO: Lockley & Peterson, 2002.

Magnussen, W.E. et al. "Reproduction." *in Crocodiles and Alligators,* C.A. Ross and S. Garrett (eds.): 118–135. New York: Facts on File, 1989.

Makovicky, P. and Currie, P. "The Presence of a Furcula in Tyrannosaurid Theropods, and Its Phylogenetic and Functional Implications." *Journal of Vertebrate Paleontology* 18 (1), March 1998: 143–149.

Marieb, E.N. and Mallatt, J. *Human Anatomy.* Redwood City, CA: The Benjamin/Cummings Publishing Company, Inc., 1992.

Marsh, O.C. "Notice of New Reptiles from the Laramie Formation." *in American Journal of Science* 43, 1892: 449–453.

Mazzotti, F. "Structure and Function." *in Crocodiles and Alligators,* C.A. Ross, S. Garrett, and T. Pyrzakowski, (eds.): 43–57. New York: Facts on File, 1989.

McGowan, C. *The Dragon Seekers.* Cambridge, MA: Perseus Publishing, 2001.

_____. *T. Rex to Go: Build Your Own from Chicken Bones.* New York: HarperCollins Publishers, 1999.

Mikhailov, K., Sabath, K., and Kurzanov, S. "Eggs and Nests from the Cretaceous of Mongolia." *in Dinosaur Eggs and Babies,* K. Carpenter, K.F. Hirsch, and J.R. Horner (eds.): 88–115. Cambridge, MA: Cambridge University Press, 1994.

Mills, M.G.L. "The Comparative Behavioral Ecology of Hyenas: The Importance of Diet and Food Dispersion." *in Carnivore Behavior, Ecology and Evolution,* J.L. Gittleman (ed.): 125–142. Ithaca, NY: Cornell University Press, 1989.

Molnar, R.E. "The Cranial Morphology of *Tyrannosaurus rex.*" Stuttgart: *Palaeontographica* 217 (1991): 137–176 & 15 plates.

Moore, J. *An Introduction to the Invertebrates.* Cambridge, England: Cambridge University Press, 2001.

Moratella, J. J. and Powell, J. E. "Dinosaur Nesting Patterns." *in Dinosaur Eggs and Babies,* K. Carpenter, K.F. Hirsch and J.R. Horner (eds.): 37–46. Cambridge, MA: Cambridge University Press, 1994.

Morrell, V. "The Origin of Birds: The Dinosaur Debate." *Audubon,* March/April 1997: 36–45.

The Nature Companions: Rocks, Fossils, and Dinosaurs. San Francisco, CA: Fog City Press, 2002.

Newman, B.H. "Stance and Gait in the Flesh Eating Dinosaur, *Tyrannosaurus.*" *Biological Journal of the Linnaean Society* 2 (2), 1970: 119–123.

Norton, O. R. *Rocks from Space: Meteorites and Meteorite Hunters.* Missoula, MT: Mountain Press Publishing Co., 1994.

< 203 >

Osborn, H.F. "*Tyrannosaurus* and other Cretaceous Carnivorous Dinosaurs." New York: American Museum of Natural History Bulletin 21, 1905: 259–265.

_____. "*Tyrannosaurus*, Upper Cretaceous Carnivorous Dinosaur (Second Communication)." New York: American Museum of Natural History Bulletin 22, 1906: 281–296.

_____. "The Crania of *Tyrannosaurus* and *Allosaurus*." New York: American Museum of Natural History Memoirs, New Series No. 1 (1), 1912: 1–30.

_____. "The skeleton of *Tyrannosaurus rex*." New York: American Museum of Natural History Bulletin 35, 1916: 762–771.

Ostrom, J.H. "*Archaeopteryx* and the Origin of Birds." London: *Biological Journal of the Linnaean Society* 8, 1976: 91–182.

Paul, G.S. *Predatory Dinosaurs of the World: A Complete Illustrated Guide*. New York: Simon and Schuster, 1988.

Psihoyos, L. *Hunting Dinosaurs*. New York: Random House, 1994.

Raath, M.A. "Morphological Variation in Small Theropods." *in Dinosaur Systematics*, K. Carpenter and P.J. Currie (eds.): 91–105. Cambridge, MA: Cambridge University Press, 1990.

Richardson, J. *The Museum of Natural History*, Vol I. London: William MacKenzie, circa 1860.

Roadside Geology Series. Missoula, MT: Mountain Press Publishing Company, various dates.

Russell, D.A. "Tyrannosaurs from the Late Cretaceous of Western Canada." *Paleontology* 1, 1970: 1–34.

Schweitzer, M.H. and Cano, R.J. "Will Dinosaurs Rise Again?" *in Dinofest: Proceedings of a Conference for the General Public*, D. Wolberg and G. Rosenburg (eds.): 309–326. Knoxville, TN: Department of Geological Sciences, The University of Tennessee, 1994.

Sternberg, C.M. *Hunting Dinosaurs in the Badlands of the Red Deer River, Alberta, Canada*. Lawrence, KS: World Company Press, 1917.

Taylor, T.G. "How an Egg Shell Is Made." *Scientific American* 222 (3), 1970: 88–95.

Thulborn, R.A. "Speeds and Gaits of Dinosaurs." *Palaeogeography, Palaeoclimatology, Palaeoecology* 38, 1982: 227–256.

Verricchio, D.J., Jackson, F., Borkowsk, J.J., and Horner, J.R. "Nest and Egg Clutches of the Dinosaur *Troodon formosus* and the Evolution of Avian Reproductive Tracts." *Nature* 385, 1997: 247–250.

"Vultures: The Carrion Gang." *in Nigel's Wild, Wild World*, Discovery Channel, 12 November 2001.

Webster, D. "Dinosaurs of the Gobi: Unearthing a Fossil Trove." *National Geographic* 190 (1), 1996: 70–89.

Weishampel, D.B., *et al.*, eds. *The Dinosauria*. Berkeley, CA: University of California Press, 1990.

Weishampel, D. and Young, L. *Dinosaurs of the East Coast*. Baltimore, MD: The Johns Hopkins University Press, 1996.

Wellnhofer, P. *The Illustrated Encyclopedia of Pterosaurs*. London: Salamander Books Limited, 1991.

Welty, J.C. and Baptista, L. *The Life of Birds*, Fourth Edition. Fort Worth: Saunders College Publishing, 1988.

Whitmer, L.M. "The Extant Phylogenetic Bracket and the Importance of Reconstructing Soft Tissues in Fossils." *in Functional Morphology in Vertebrate Paleontology*. J. Thomason (ed.): 19–33. Cambridge, MA: Cambridge University Press, 1995.

< 204 >